Romantic Fantasy and Science Fiction

Romantic Fantasy
and
Science Fiction

KARL KROEBER

Yale University Press
New Haven and London

Designed by James J. Johnson
and set in Electra types by TCSystems, Shippensburg, Penn.
Printed in the United States of America by
Vail-Ballou Press, Binghamton, N.Y.

Library of Congress Cataloging-in-Publication Data

Kroeber, Karl, 1926–
    Romantic fantasy and science fiction/Karl Kroeber.
        p.   cm.
    Bibliography: p.
    Includes index.
    ISBN 0–300–04241–8 (alk. paper)
    1. Romanticism.   2. Fantastic literature—History and criticism.
3. Science fiction—History and criticism.   4. Love in literature.
I. Title.
PN603.K76 1988
809.3'876—dc 19   88–2046
                                                                CIP

The paper in this book meets the guidelines for
permanence and durability of the Committee on
Production Guidelines for Book Longevity of the
Council on Library Resources

1   3   5   7   9   10   8   6   4   2

TO

Kishamish,

my fantasy

Contents

CHAPTER ONE

Romantic Fantasy

> The role of art, then, is primarily to express the complex of human existence, humanity's awareness of being itself rather than its perception of what is not itself and is outside it.
>
> NORTHROP FRYE, *The Stubborn Structure*

OMANTIC FANTASY EMERGES OUT OF ENLIGHTEN-
ment culture, which excluded anything fantastic from civilized life. Romantic fantasy celebrates the magical in a society for which magic had become only benighted superstition. The essential mode of Romantic fantastic discourse, therefore, derives from the trope of oxymoron—an impossible possibility. Use of this mode necessarily involves the fantasist in an art of intense self-reflexivity, enchanting himself so that he may enchant others. This inwardness distinguishes fantasy from its nonidentical twin, science fiction. Science fiction also appears when the supernatural has been driven out of enlightened society, but instead of seeking to recover otherness and magicality, science fiction extrapolates consequences of the scientific-technological progress that destroyed superstition.

In the chapter following this introductory one, centered on Mary Shelley's *Frankenstein*, the prototypical work of science fiction, I explore implications of the distinction between science fiction and fantasy. I then focus on Coleridge's "Rime of the Ancient Mariner" and Keats's "La Belle Dame Sans Merci." In chapter 4 I contrast Keats's poem to both other literary ballads and "authentic" popular ballads to illuminate how Romantic fantasy uncovers qualities obscured or elided in genuine balladry

1

and undesired by later nineteenth-century and Modern poets. Chapter 5 juxtaposes "The Rime of the Ancient Mariner" with Robert Browning's "Childe Roland to the Dark Tower Came" to deepen understanding of how and why Romantic fantasy was exorcised from the mainstream of nineteenth- and twentieth-century literature, an exorcism culminating in Freud's essay on "The Uncanny."

In chapter 6 I describe the un-Freudian psychology that made possible creations of Romantic fantasy, analyzing Keats's "Ode to Psyche," with special attention to one of the poem's sources, *The Golden Ass* of Apuleius, a work having good claim to being the premier fantasy of classical antiquity. Through discussion of Heinrich von Kleist's *Michael Kohlhass*, the final chapter demonstrates the necessity for stylistic radicalism in fantasy's self-challenging forms, suggesting that the recent revival of critical interest in fantasy reflects postmodern literature's concern with self-contesting structures, as is illustrated by Gabriel García Márquez's "The Last Voyage of the Ghost Ship."

Postmodernism's return toward Romantic inspiration is impressive because of fantasy's bare survival in marginal forms throughout the era of Modernism. As the modernist aesthetic's hostility to fantasy as serious art—revealed most disturbingly in the Modern invention of the "primitive" (see chapter 5)—began to wane in the early sixties, a revival of fantastic literature and fruitful criticism of it became possible. Contributors to this transformation, not surprisingly, came with diverse motives and even more diverse foci of attention. Most were not mainstream figures either in the world of the arts or of academic criticism. Bakhtin, of course, was one, and his obscurity until recent years is now legendary. Another was Tolkien, the respectability of whose fiction and criticism alike still are suspect among celebrated movers and shakers in academia. But Tolkien's essay "On Fairy Stories," first published in 1947, articulates some essential qualities of fantasy more cogently than many later and more pretentious essays.[1] However one evaluates Tolkien's fiction, one must recognize that, unlike most commentators on the fantastic, he worked hard at creating fantasy himself, and he thought long and deeply about medieval literature, especially

Beowulf. Tolkien remains almost unique among critics of the fantastic in having read lovingly in pre-Renaissance literatures wherein fantasy functions powerfully.

It might be difficult to name a writer more unlike Tolkien than Jean Paul Sartre, but he, too, signaled the coming revaluations of fantasy. Sartre perceived that Romantic fantasy appears with the triumph of secularized culture, and that it is a literature necessarily without conclusive and definitive meanings, since it does not serve transcendental purposes. Beyond these valid observations, however, he did not advance because for him fantasy must represent the happy triumph of the purely human:

> There are no phantoms, no succubi, no weeping fountains. There are only men, and the creator of the fantastic announces that he identifies himself with the fantastic object.[2]

To the contrary, fantasy originates in the possibility of an authentic otherness. The fantastic is exactly what one cannot identify with, something that is not mankind as mankind knows itself. Romantic fantasy is a protest against exactly the total humanization of life that Sartre applauds. Fantasy becomes necessary, as Bakhtin understood, when, with the dismantling of all supernaturalism men find themselves imprisoned in a totally rationalized humanism, one that threatens them with self-dehumanization.

Tzvetan Todorov's book *The Fantastic* is especially interesting because when Todorov wrote it he was committed to a rigorously structuralist approach that might have disabled his critique. But by 1970 a revision in established attitudes toward fantastic literature was becoming inevitable, and Todorov succeeds in focusing on some core issues in this literature. Part of the strength of his work depends on his intellectual awareness of Eastern European traditions, for his key insights are adapted from Russian writers and critics, notably Dostoyevsky. Most of those who have followed Todorov, especially among the French, have lacked this background and so have been poorly equipped to develop his work's most significant implications.

Perhaps the simplest fashion of illustrating the usefulness of Todorov's book is to single out the most problematic assertion in his basic definition of fantasy.

> The fantastic . . . lasts only as long as a certain hesitation: a hesitation common to reader and character, who must decide whether or not what they perceive derives from "reality" as it exists in common opinion. At the story's end, the reader makes a decision even if the character does not; he opts for one solution or the other, and thereby emerges from the fantastic. If he decides that the laws of reality remain intact and permit an explanation of the phenomena described, we say that the work belongs to another genre: the uncanny. If, on the contrary, he decides that new laws of nature must be entertained to account for the phenomena, we enter the genre of the marvelous.
>
> The fantastic therefore leads a life full of dangers, and may evaporate at any moment.[3]

As has by now often been observed, there is a problem in Todorov's term "hesitation," suggested by his need to proliferate categories at once, distinguishing the fantastic from the uncanny and the marvelous. The fantastic, he insists, can be recognized uniquely by that "hesitation experienced by a person who knows only the laws of nature, confronting an apparently supernatural event"(Todorov, 25). But as normally defined, "hesitation" seems the wrong term for the effect of fantasy's impossible realities. No more than the dragon in *Beowulf* does García Márquez' ghost ship "twenty times taller than the steeple and some ninety-seven times longer than the village" leave room for hesitation. The ghost ship presents to "gaping disbelievers" the impasse of an indisputably impossible actuality. Hesitancy, one is tempted to say, is exactly what effective fantasy does not permit. Yet if we recognize that Todorov is working within constrictive formalistic assumptions and premises of Freudian psychology, we can legitimately interpret his "hesitation" as implying something much like that "discourse through oxymoron" that truly constitutes fantasy. Analogously, his observation on the evanescing of fantasy points to an important truth: fantasy does appear gratuitously, presenting something quite unneeded by the society into which it intrudes, because it is *other*. As we shall see, Romantic fantasy indeed thrusts itself into an environment hostile even to conceiving the possibility of its existence.

Because virtually all major commentators on fantastic literature following Todorov have sought to rectify the weaknesses of his analyses, we need not dwell on them but should rather give him credit for inspiring different approaches that refined and improved on his pioneering effort. Theodore Ziolkowsky, for example, in *Images of Enchantment* meticulously traces out three fantastic images recurrent in Western literature from antiquity to the present to demonstrate that Todorov's synchronic genres are better understood in a "diachronic sequence."[4] C. N. Manlove, less committed to so purely a chronological method, brings under survey a wider and more diversified range of literature than Todorov to arrive at a general definition of fantasy advancing some of Tolkien's fundamental insights.

> A fantasy is: a fiction evoking wonder and containing a substantial and irreducible element of the supernatural with which the mortal characters in the story or readers become on at least partly familiar terms.[5]

Manlove's formation, transforming Todorov's "hesitation" into "becoming familiar with," remains the best succinct definition of fantasy, and his application of it to particular works is consistently tactful and acute; indeed, one hopes that he will develop some of the more provacative implications of his definition, for neither of the two best subsequent commentators on fantasy have adequately taken his work into account.

Both Rosemary Jackson and Tobin Siebers, whose books to date stand as the most intellectually significant studies of fantasy, are not—for different reasons, Jackson because of her Marxian-Freudian bias, Siebers because of his Girardian slant— sympathetic to Manlove's Tolkienian line of inquiry. Jackson, drawing shrewdly on the work of critics such as Irwin, Russ, and Bessière, as well as Todorov, writes the first study to give adequate prominence to the fantastic's focus on "that which cannot be, but is."[6] She realizes that this requires the style of fantasy to be oxymoronic to match its antinomic structure, so that fantasy is incapable on any level of progression toward synthesis. Although she cannot finally integrate Bakhtin's insights to her dependence on psychoanalysis, she recognizes the importance of the Russian's perception of fantasy as a primary dialogical form. She seems uncertain, though, as to what in fact constitutes dialogical form, a topic on which I try to shed some light in chapter 5.

Like most commentators on the fantastic, especially those under the spell of Freud, Jackson has difficulty in dealing with the "natural" and "supernatural," and with how to challenge the validity of the assumption that the "real" and the "imaginary" are simple, self-explanatory opposites, though the direction of her argument points to the need for such challenge.

Tobin Siebers, who has a better grasp than Jackson both of the metaphysical roots of the diverse critical methods now popular in the study of the fantastic and of their ethical and intellectual implications, demonstrates the necessity for a critic of fantasy carefully to define the meaning of "supernaturalism," which implies particularly the need to define, with a specificity recommended by Bakhtin, the nature of any particular fantasy's audience.[7] Siebers understands that when we talk about fantasy today, we in fact refer almost exclusively to the "Romantic fantastic," that is, works resulting from the Western European Enlightenment's demolition of faith in the supernatural. He understands, therefore, that Romantic fantasy expresses an immediate reaction against the triumph of humanizing and rationalizing culture at the end of the eighteenth century. And aware of the relevance of René Girard's studies in the relation of violence and culture, Siebers astutely identifies the most powerful impulse within Romantic fantasy as its effort to regain the viewpoint of the superstititous. Romantic fantasy is a protest against the violence of enlightened, rationalized, Voltairean society that makes superstition one of its principal victims. Siebers thus is able to explain the paradox of fantasy's appearance in a society that had officially and happily banished the fantastic, why Romantic writers "sought to believe what they could no longer believe."[8]

Siebers' work, even more clearly than that of Jackson, Manlove, and Todorov, points toward a conclusion he does not explicitly enunciate, partly because of the texts and artists he chooses to concentrate on: the Romantic fantastic is a mode of turning critical skepticism against itself. Romantic fantasy in so doing seeks not to destroy skepticism but to define its limits, so that the monstrous conditions of rationally mechanized society can at least be meliorated. Romantic fantasy is not, as Rosemary Jackson thinks, nostalgic. To the contrary, it desires to improve a present situation that has become intolerable through the obliterating of any otherness in a world human beings have come to dominate with frightening completeness. Because of this paradox, as Siebers' work demonstrates persuasively, serious criticism of fantastic literature cannot be merely formalistic, if only because a subject of its inquiries is the skeptical intelligence on which formalistic analysis depends. Fantasy, therefore, has become especially interesting to poststructuralist critics and attractive to today's general readers in expressing resistance not to some particular ideology but to underlying cultural attitudes that have produced the oppressive antihuman character of all contemporary ideologies.

This book attempts to extend and more precisely articulate the implications in recent studies of fantastic literature, as well as to develop some specific insights into exactly how and why it originated as it did. My basic technique for doing this is to concentrate on English Romantics, Mary Shelley, Coleridge, and Keats, so as to rectify an important omission in recent criticism, which has focused on continental literatures. As I point out in chapter 4, the English Romantics reacting against the violence of Enlightenment rationality could with justice believe, unlike any of their continental contemporaries, that in writing fantasy they were recovering a major feature of their finest literary tradition. The English Romantics were confident that in engaging in fantasy they followed a path laid out by Shakespeare, the greatest of all literary artists.

By devoting attention to *Frankenstein* as a means of discriminating science fiction from fantasy, furthermore, I can dramatize how it was the the triumph of humanism that disenchanted Western culture. Until we recognize that Romantic fantasy is an effort to restore balance to a world distorted by its total conquest by humankind, we cannot understand the essential nature of this literary mode—nor why today fantasy revives simultaneously with a rejection of literary artistry and literary criticism founded on traditional humanism. Finally, we must learn to perceive how modern psychology, Freudian psychology, dominant in Western society in this century, necessarily works against either the creation or appreciation of fantasy. Until we develop sympathy for psychological concepts very different from those which we have so internalized that we have difficulty subjecting them to effective critical analysis, we cannot valorize fantasy's special kind of discourse. The nature of the psychology making possible fantasy is revealed by Keats's "Ode to Psyche," a poem not usually associated with this topic. But when we compare and contrast the ode with one of the great fantastic works of antiquity that is a source for Keats's poem, we can perceive how fantasy might function as a recuperative mode of literature in post-Enlightenment culture. Analogously, the fantastic elements in *Michael Kohlhaas* have not heretofore been adequately assessed. Carefully examined, these compel us to realize the limitations of much formalistic criticism for dealing with those stylistic complexities integral to fantastic art, especially those resulting from its essentially self-conflicting character, produced as a means of displaying the limitations of literary "realism." This is why, finally, an understanding of fantastic art is perhaps the best means of appreciating the central purposes of some of the most exciting recent novelists such as Gabriel Garcia Márquez. Just as Romantic fantasy recovered to reshape interlinked psychological concepts and stylistic techniques from a disavowed social and literary past, so we can gain a sense for an efficacy of literature in contempory life if we are willing to appreciate the validity of its confrontation with our era's accelerating homogenization of cultural differences, and even differences between individuals, *difference* having been the foundation of Romantic fantasy.

CHAPTER TWO

Science Fiction vs. Fantasy

Pardon this intrusion.

FIRST ARTICULATE SPEECH OF
FRANKENSTEIN'S MONSTER.

HE GENRES OF SCIENCE FICTION AND FANTASY OVER-
lap and interpenetrate. All literary genres are
impure, each partaking of diverse formal
modalities, but fantasy and science fiction are
especially interwined because they have a
common origin.[1] Yet only by recognizing
how they differ can we understand the significance of their opposite responses to the triumphant humanizing
of Western post-Renaissance culture. All commentators on science fiction (and this is a substantial number, for of currently
popular literary genres it is the one most systematically analyzed,
cataloged, classified,—in a word, most scientifically studied)
agree that the key to the genre is *extrapolation*.[2] The writer of
science fiction extends or projects or draws inferences from what
is known and accepted (and the primary known fact of the
modern world is that humanity dominates our globe). The
science fiction writer extrapolates scientifically, of course, which
means that he or she employs the basic style of scientific
discourse—analytical, reportorial exposition: his basic form is
scientific reportage.[3]

Fantasy responds to the same circumstance of humanity's
technological triumph differently, leading some critics to think
of fantasy simply as a looking backward. But fantasy, although
it may try to recover a lost sense for otherness, turns inward

9

rather than backward. Fantasy is a primary form of literary self-reflexivity. It explores the deepest implications of oxymoron rather than attempting extrapolation. Fantasy involves its author is self-enchantment, which leads the fantasist toward a discourse distinct from the realistic, rationalistic, expository forms that undergird science fiction. Fantasy tends toward self-involuting procedures, and these often result in complex structures parallel to, though totally distinct from, the intricacies of earlier narrational modes, such as the Beowulfian interlacings to which I refer below. But Romantic fantasy is not nostalgic, for it arises from consciousness of a need to go beyond earlier, simpler, less self-contesting beliefs in the possibility of otherness. Romantic fantasy can only use earlier modes for inspiration, as means for focusing the skeptical intelligence on which scientific, technological thinking is founded against itself, thus deliberately and self-consciously creating a reality it understands to be impossible.

THE BEOWULFIAN MONSTER

Most of the multitude of critics of science fiction treat Mary Shelley's *Frankenstein* (1818) as the premier prototype of the twentieth-century genre.[4] Besides making use of the most exciting advanced science of its day, the novel introduces the best-known of the many modern monsters who in science fiction so often replace the commonplace human figures of nineteenth-century realistic fiction. The "monster" is a key feature of science fiction. In earlier literature monsters are rare. Among the ugly few in our tradition Caliban is the most famous, but Grendel in *Beowulf* most illuminatingly contrasts with Shelley's creature. The contrast is especially attractive because when Shelley wrote she knew nothing of Grendel, since *Beowulf* had not yet been rescued by scholarship from its profound obscurity.

Appropriately enough, Grendel inhabits a mist-shrouded borderland, and his appearance is not distinctly visualized, although his habitat is hauntingly evoked.[5]

> Mysterious is the region
> They live in—of wolf-fells, wind-picked moors
> And treacherous fen-paths; a torrent of water

> pours down dark cliffs and plunges into the earth,
> an underground flood. It is not far from here,
> in terms of miles, that the Mere lies,
> overcast with dark, crag-rooted trees
> that hang in groves hoary with frost.
> An uncanny sight may be seen at night there
> —the fire in the water! . . .
>
> . . . .
>
> And the wind can stir up wicked storms there,
> whipping the swirling waters up
> till they climb the clouds and clog the air,
> making the skies weep. (94)

Grendel's "terrible, fearsome" nature is mysterious, except that, because he is linked to Satan and Cain—some of his epithets are "fiend in hell" (1012) and "demon in hell" (1247a)—he is unmistakably evil. These features distinguish Grendel from some prominent monsters of classical Mediterranean cultures, say the Medusa, or the Cyclops who appears in the *Odyssey*. These Grecian monsters are delineated clearly and decisively situated: they are not borderlanders. Even their family connections are well established, Polyphemus, for instance, being respectably related to Poseidon. Nor, though dangerous and destructively frightful, are these creatures presented as evil in the way Grendel is. Medusa and Polyphemus, of course, are pre-Christian. But in part so too is Grendel, for his marginality and indistinctness arise from spiritual as well as geographical sources.

Grendel's chilling dangerousness is deepened and complicated by his Teutonic heritage: Hrothgar regards him as an intruder, but Grendel may have a better claim to being indigenous. Grendel, in fact, concretizes the intermixing of Christian and pagan cultures which *Beowulf* as a whole so superbly dramatizes, so superbly that scholars continue to quarrel violently over the dialectical clashing.[6] Suffice it to say here that no other poem enables us to feel more keenly how diverse cultures can combine, thereby reminding us that most societies in fact support "impure" cultures consisting of layerings of distinct ways of life.

Indeed, if one has ever wondered, as I have, how Christianity could so successfully have imposed itself on the vigor of Germanic peoples, *Beowulf* may be especially illuminating, its final lines, for example, epitomizing the process:

> They said that he was of all the world's kings
> the gentlest of men, and the most gracious,
> the kindest to his people, the keenest for fame. (151)

Beowulf is heroic both in a pagan, physical sense and in a Christian, spiritual sense, for he is a killer who is kind. Unlike classical epic heroes who are heroic because they succeed, Beowulf's heroism incorporates a final crushing failure into his victory so that his heroism calls itself into question, thereby adding a tragic dimension to the heroic. As Arthur Brodeur says:

> It is more than the death of Beowulf which constitutes
> the tragedy . . . his tragedy is that he dies in vain . . .
> his death brings in its train the overthrow of his people.[7]

That the tragic aspect of his career owes most to sources in German mythology is suggested by the circumstance that his great battles are not against men but against monsters, Grendel and his mother, and the nonmonstrous but totally alien dragon. And Beowulf himself is represented as a bearlike man in whose hands the best swords shatter. He thus retains, as Aeneas, Odysseus, and Achilles do not, direct links with natural conditions only partially overcome by the cultural achievements of his society, though in its technology and sociological complexity his society is richer than that celebrated in the Homeric poems.

Beowulf, unlike the heroes of Greek and Roman epic, literally grapples with the ahuman. Because he does so, his story resonates with the peculiar potency of a Germanic mythological system in which men and gods together struggle against strange if natural beings of another kind, even to final mutual destruction. Such undertones throughout *Beowulf* endow with powerful complexity the poem's seemingly oversimple Christian morality that pits unqualified goodness against indisputable evil, the godly against the satanic.

Thematic and structural intricacy enable us to imagine how

seemingly antagonistic systems may interact and become mutually reinforcing. Grendel is profoundly evil because his links to Satan and Cain simultaneously reflect his connection to the dark forces which threatened Asgard, whose fate was finally Beowulf's, violent destruction. Even if one insists that there may be implicit in his death a redemptive idealism foreign to Teutonic mythology, Beowulf's virtue at best is complicated, partaking of diverse, even contradictory, systems of ideals. And the threat posed by his monstrous antagonists is as complicated.

It is not surprising, then, that the poem possesses a remarkably intricate form of structural and thematic self-crossings, an interlacing of antitheses so that diversly intersecting macro and micro oppositions simultaneously contrast and parallel, both reflect and refract one another. It is appropriate that, unlike the Homeric dactylic hexameter and its Latin successor, *Beowulf's* basic metrical unit is two unequal half-lines joined by similar initial sounds in two or three syllables, its line thus shaped with irregular regularity around a caesura, a gap in sound, a silence, an absence. This key linear emptiness, as Tolkien I believe first suggested, is magnified into the fifty-year silence in the narrative line that contains the untold story of Beowulf's successful reign, a silence crucial to the linkage, both linear and cyclical, of elements of the poem's opening section to its conclusion, contrastive parallelism emphasized by the funerals which begin and end the poem and concretize how it dramatizes simultaneous success and defeat. And of course the untold history in the narrative line occurs slightly off center, past the poem's midpoint, so that the whole is constituted by two unequal though interreflecting parts. Such internal symmetry of asymmetry between theme and form recurs in every one of the work's structural systems, most impressively in the intertwining by which stories weave into and out of one another, one temporarily obscuring another as it crosses over it, and even different phases of the same narrative overlapping itself, as events and the telling of events interlace to create a unique vision of a society not merely existing but also being imagined, so that both its past and its future are always darkly but portentously imaged in its present. On the microcosmic level of word and line the poem is

most powerful when most self-involuting, as when Heorot is
imagined destroyed even as being built.

> Boldly the hall reared
> its arched gables; unkindled the torch-flame
> that turned it to ashes. (53)

Equivalent formal-thematic catachreses recur throughout the
macrostructure of episodes, perhaps most strikingly in the depiction of the defeat and dispersion of Beowulf's people after his
fatal triumph over the dragon.

> No fellow shall wear
> an arm ring in his memory; no maiden's neck
> shall be enhanced in beauty by the bearing of these
>   rings.
> Bereft of gold, rather, and in wretchedness of mind
> she shall tread continually the tracks of exile
> now that the leader of armies has laid aside his mirth,
> his sport and glad laughter. Many spears shall
>   therefore
> feel cold in the mornings to the clasping fingers
> and the hands that raise them. Nor shall the harper's
>   melody
> arouse them for battle; and yet the black raven
> quick on the marked men, shall have much to
>   speak of
> when he tells the eagle of his takings at the feast
> where he and the wolf bared the bodies of the slain.
>   (146–47)

FRANKENSTEIN'S MONSTER

I have hastily enumerated some aspects of *Beowulf's* artistry
because the poem's structures and deployments of thematic
strategies stand in the starkest contrast to systems of science
fiction, the contrast providing efficient means for understanding
the nature and function of the later genre. *Frankenstein*, for

example, is truly prototypical of later science fiction precisely in owing so little, substantively or stylistically, to earlier epic and romance. Shelley's work is closely bound to the forms of realistic prose fiction, forms that dominated later eighteenth- and early nineteenth-century European literature. Epical or romance modes of discourse diverge from those favored in science fiction, because these poetic genres tend away from the simple lucidity of language toward which scientific discourse aspires. As Aldous Huxley puts it, the scientist "uses the vocabulary and syntax of common speech in such a way that each phrase is susceptible of only one interpretation."[8] Or, as Parrinder observes, predisposed toward the style of reportage,[9] science fiction regularly avoids complexity of form, especially the complexity, I would add, so intriguingly manifest in Beowulfian circling self-intersections. Science fiction's stylistic simplicity is illuminated by the nature of its monsters, of which *Frankenstein*'s is one of the more memorable. Science fiction monsters tend not to be borderland creatures, only temporarily mysterious, and seldom unequivocally evil (however dangerous)—in short, un-Grendelian. The nature of modern monstrousness is quite different from that frightful otherness Grendel embodies, as is revealed by the central portion of Shelley's novel, chapters 11 through 15, the segment usually eliminated from dramatizations, in which the monster's education is detailed.[10]

In these chapters Shelley's garrulous creature persuades Victor Frankenstein that he is not, like Grendel, naturally evil, but has been educated into murderousness. As I listen to the monster, I am tempted to regard him as a victim of the myth of the noble savage, for his autobiography is a conventionalized representation of why the self-consciousness demanded by advanced society is a blighting curse, not a blessing. Describing his gradual acquiring of skill in using his senses, for example, he reports that originally he was intensely responsive to the beauties of nature, so uncorrupted that of his first pastoral meal he enjoyed all but the wine (101). His own needs are so benignly simple that he cannot at first understand why the cottagers, whom he secretly watches and learns from, regret the loss of unnecessary luxuries. Nature seems to him so bountiful that even their level of retired life breeds superfluous desires. As he goes on observing the bucolic existence of Felix, Agatha, and their father, the monster's sentiments evolve generously: his empathy with their joys and sorrows is entirely benevolent. When he comprehends that his innocent stealing has caused the cottagers pain, he becomes self-sacrificing and labors to provide selflessly for their needs (106). Sensually, emotionally, morally he is, so he tells his maker, naturally pure, kind, good.

Corruption results from the development of the monster's reasoning intellect. He begins as a natural poet delighting in the songs of birds (99), and he is delighted when first exposed to the cottagers singing and playing. But when he hears prose read aloud he describes it, ominously, as "sounds that were monotonous" (104). When he learns French, he is taught to his dismay by Volney's *Ruins of Empires* that human societies are distinguished by artibrary social inequities, and that men are usually esteemed only for their wealth, social position, or physical beauty (p. 114). These observations turn the creature's mind to self-reflection. He realizes with agony that poor, outcast, and ugly as he is he cannot expect to be esteemed by mankind. Miserable, he wishes he had never left his uncultivated condition and that he could forget his learning. And the more he advances in knowledge, the more he is afflicted. *The Sorrows of Young Werther* teaches him to anticipate emotional isolation because of his acute sensibility, while *Paradise Lost* suggests that although he may be a type of Adam, because he possesses no chance of redemption, he is closer to the position of Satan, but even more painfully situated than the archfiend because he lacks companions in woe (p. 124). Growing self-awareness encourages growing self-loathing. His self-alienation is climaxed by the cottagers' horrified rejection of him. The creature had dared to hope his refined sensibility, keen intellect, and benevolent feelings would attract their sympathy, for he knows that they themselves have undergone unjustified suffering. But they are revolted by his physical appearance. So culture, intellect, and civilized sensibilities lead to the destruction of his naturally good, kindly, pure being and turn him into a monster.

VICTOR FRANKENSTEIN AS MONSTER

The decisive event of the creature's life, then, is his rejection by human beings dwelling in rather idyllic conditions, their rejection precipitated simply by his ugliness. His deformity masks profound goodness, just as the handsomeness of the cottagers, he learns, conceals their essential timorousness and repressed rage. If we decide to believe the monster (though his tale is uncorroborated, because it is his enemy who reports his account we are not unreasonable in accepting his story), we are then compelled to wonder how accurately Victor Frankenstein's story of his idyllic upbringing accords with genuine reality. We must wonder whether his autobiography may not unconsciously reveal a deceptiveness in civilized life, if the beauty he describes may not conceal some ugly attributes, as does the ideal life of the cottagers. Victor's story, in fact, displays to us, though not to him, why and how respectable bourgeois society produces creators of monstrousness.

Of reciprocal understanding, let alone love, there is scarcely a trace in the noncommunicating Frankenstein family, whom we are told are leading figures in Geneva's commercial society. Victor's father saves Caroline Beaufort, because their society allows a woman no means to support herself, and her father dies because of his shame at his mere bad luck in mercantile ventures, a shame that apparently prevents him from perceiving how selfishly he ruins his daughter's existence. Any doubts about the older Frankenstein's true motives in marrying Caroline are erased when the happy couple in effect buy Elizabeth Lavenza as a "pretty present" (35) for Victor, justifying their action by comtemplating the advantages they thus bestow on her, a most dubious one being betrothal to Victor. Victor aptly describes Elizabeth as the "inmate of my parent's house" (18), but being prisoner there may be better than being subjected to his possessive affection: "I . . . looked upon Elizabeth as mine—mine to protect, love, and cherish. All praises bestowed on her I received as made to a possession of my own." (35).

The true quality of Frankensteinian affection and responsibility is dramatized by the family's effective abandonment of

Justine, a faithful servant wrongly accused of the murder of
William on the basis of flimsy evidence. Despite her long service
to the family and the absence of serious motive, Victor's father,
while professing confidence in her innocence, does nothing to
save her. He urges Elizabeth (who, not being a Frankenstein, is
passionately concerned for Justine and tries to act in her behalf)
to "rely on the justice of our laws"—which promptly condemn
the innocent girl to death—"and the activity with which I shall
prevent the slightest shadow of partiality" (77). The meaning of
his final phrase appears in his, and Victor's, failure to speak any
word at the public trial in defense of Justine's character. This
nonaction disguised by specious concern for judicious procedures is of a piece with the placing by Victor's father over the
mantelpiece in his drawing room a painting he had commis-
sioned of Caroline Beaufort "in an agony of despair; kneeling by
the coffin of her dead father" (75). Presumably this charming
memento will keep his "beloved" wife mindful of how much she
owes to him.

The Frankensteins produce a full-blown monster in Victor,
who climactically manifests the family's morbid traits. In a
manner worthy of his father he extols calm rationality, "a human
being in perfection ought always to preserve a calm and peaceful
mind and never allow passion or a transitory desire to disturb his
tranquility." (54), while behaving with uncontrolled violence. He
becomes obsessed with his monster, obsessed because he refuses
to acknowledge it openly, resists confronting the reality of his
relation to it. He creates the monster with little thought of any
consequences beyond that of securing his fame and the gratitude
he would be able to "claim from those he created" (52, 53). He
literally rushes away from the creature as soon as he has
produced it, frightened by behavior that to a neutral observer
seems an appeal for comfort and affection. Thereafter Victor
tries to forget the creature completely. He tries so hard that he
finds it virtually impossible to speak of it. He passionately desires
to believe that the monster does not actually exist, that it is but a
produce of his imagining. Victor's attitude produces disastrous
consequences, but it is exactly that of most modern critics, of
whom Harold Bloom is representative when he observes that "the

monster and his creator are antithetical halves of a single being."[11] Bloom thus accomplishes for Victor the derealization Victor desires, in effect, denying the reality of his responsibility to another being—a leading trait of the Frankenstein family.[12]

Mary Shelley's novel is prototypical of subsequent science fiction because it represents so powerfully how our modern, scientific, technological society dehumanizes itself—even in its literary criticism. In *Frankenstein* one observes how human beings have become the sole—but quite sufficient—threat to humanity, self-destroyers through their own creations. And the essential modernity of Mary Shelley's vision is nowhere plainer than at the climax of Victor's scientific career, when he decides finally not to make a mate for the monster. One could say that he may be Oppenheimer but will not be Teller, because Frankenstein's motive for deconstructing his female monster is concern for the survival of his species.

> Even if they [monster and mate] were to leave Europe and inhabit the deserts of the new world, yet one of the first results of those sympathies for which the demon thirsted would be children, and a race of devils would be propagated upon the earth who might make the very existence of the species of man a condition precarious and full of terror. Had I right, for my own benefit, to inflict this curse upon everlasting generations? . . . I shuddered to think that future ages might curse me as their pest, whose selfishness had not hesitated to buy its own peace at the price, perhaps, of the existence of the whole human race. (158–59)

Frankenstein thinks of neither his family nor local community, because in fact neither for him have any reality. He thinks in terms of self and race. But given the self-deceptions in his social and domestic behavior, one is forced to look skeptically at his claim of noble motive, which is an appeal, after all, to an abstraction. The very force of the monster's argument that his singleness makes him monstrous should cause us to reflect that a person such as Frankenstein, a self-isolating being apparently incapable of meaningful relations with anyone else, merely conceals his emotional impotence from himself by asserting his special responsibility to mankind at large. A man who, when the monster warns him, "I will be with you on your wedding night," ignores even the possibility of a threat to his betrothed, seems committed to socially menacing self-deception.

Frankenstein's concern for his race is the obverse of his solipsistic egoism. To define one's humanity in terms of an abstract universal such as one's species, whether the reference be biological or psychological, and not in any way in terms of what is limitedly and contingently shared with other specific individuals—the way, of course, that the monster wished to define himself—is to risk making the concept of humanity a mask for monstrous behavior. Beginning with dreams of being celebrated as a benefactor—"I should . . . pour a torrent light into our dark world. A new species would bless me as its creator and source; . . . No father could claim the gratitude of his child so completely as I should deserve theirs"(51, 52–53)—Victor concludes his idealistic account with an act, destroying the female creature, that ominously foreshadows Mr. Kurtz's epilogue to his idealistic treatise on bringing enlightenment to the African natives in *Heart of Darkness*: "Exterminate all the brutes!"

SCIENCE FICTION'S DESOCIALIZED NARRATIVE

Interpretations of Shelley's novel that treat the monster as Frankenstein's double, now perhaps the favorite interpretation, make impossible any ethical condemnation of Frankenstein. Modern critics like to define Victor as he would prefer to define himself, as victim, not as someone necessarily engaged in specific personal and particularized social responsibilities. But the cogency of the issue Shelly poses harshly—what is the validity of an appeal to the good of the species?—in our century of nuclear and chemical weapons is beyond dispute.[13] In fact, objections to the hydrogen bomb were couched in terms drawn from Shelley's novel: James B. Conant opposed construction by saying, "we built one Frankenstein."[14] An important function of science fiction, though it has been little remarked upon by literary critics, has been to pose such issues to our imagination, issues which in earlier times unafflicted and unbenefited by triumphs of scientific/technological powers, one could scarecely raise.

Once again a contrast with *Beowulf* helps to clarify the special significance of science fiction, because sociofamilial relations are so central to the Anglo-Saxon poem. Fratricide threatens the Beowulfian world at every turn, though fratricide's possible psychic causes are not explored. Feuds, which the poem represents as an extended form of the fratricidal impulse, are terrible precisely because they disintegrate the center of social relations: broken family and broken society are in *Beowulf* intrareflective. Feud, the self-conflict of the social group, is the focus of ethical issues in the poem, as appears even in its form. For *Beowulf* consists of a third-person narration by a teller never unwilling to proclaim that his story is a retelling of what he had been told by others—

> Straightway, as I have heard, the son of Weoxstan
> obeyed his wounded lord, . . .
> I heard of the plundering of the hoard in the knoll—
> 138–39

just as he begins "We have heard of the thriving," only gradually moving into first-person narration as the poem progresses. The interlocked chain of retellings of retellings that constitutes the poem iteself helps to hold society together. Public renarration is a form in which ethical self-examination and affirmation help to establish continuity of the group. Indeed, a narrative's "expressive intonation" (to use Bakhtin's terminology) reveals with peculiar clarity the actually functioning—as distinct from abstract definition of—the ethical dynamics of the society that sponsors its retelling and rereception. The teller is author of this particular telling, but the preexistent story he tells "authors" him. For such a teller solipsism is impossible.[15] *Frankenstein*, in absolute contrast, consists of an encapsulated series of solipsistic monologues, which at decisive points are linked only by coincidence. Walton's chance encounter with Frankenstein in the Arctic, for example, is meaningful chiefly through symbolic parallelism, his ambition parallels Victor's, or symbolic contrast, icy waste against cottage in verdant woods. Such thematic symbolizing reinforces our sense that what is most monstrous in the novel is neither its strange creature, nor even his diseased creator, but a basic moral incoherence in the society that produces both.

To display social incoherence pretending to sophisticated organizedness seems a driving force behind much of the best science fiction—Zamyatin's *We* being an outstanding instance. The observation helps to explain why the genre's aesthetic basis has persistently remained expository realism.[16] Science fiction appropriately uses language in unrecursive narrative forms and a direct style of reportage because it extrapolates from scientific and technological conditions favoring such modes of representation as closest to reality. The literary form adapts from its technological model an assumption of uncomplicated relations between language and what it represents. But the assumption, in fact, manifests how through science and technology humans dehumanize themselves, for a denial of the intricate dubiety of linguistic representation of either physical or psychic phenomena denigrates the complexity of human communication and the awesome diversity of its functions.

The predominant style of science fiction, then, alerts us to the profound paradox of its favored themes: it seems to deal with alien forms, monsters, Martians, green spores from Alpha Centauri, mutants in distant galaxies, and the like, but all these are in fact only means for dramatizing how our world has become so exclusively humanized as to be self-diseased. The Martians, mutants, and intelligent spores are extrapolations of our frighteningly practical imaginative power as it is expressed in a technological and scientific progress that annihilates otherness.

Mary Shelley's novel, composed of intersecting and symbolically related yet isolated narratives, foretells the essential form of science fiction as desocialized narrative. Whether employing impersonal reportage or private monologue, science fiction is a form ill suited for articulating dialogic consciousness. Again *Beowulf* supplies a handy contrast, for when in the 1970s John Gardner retold the story in *Grendel* he limited himself, or, better, the circumstances of the time limited him, to telling from Grendel's point of view. Gardner's narrative perspective, that is to say, humanizes the monster, which, of course, is to make the monstrous human. Gardner thereby dramatizes what most decisively separates science fiction from fantasy, for fantasy seeks to develop a vision of a world in which humans cohabit with nonhumans, rather than extrapolating, as science fiction does, contemporary processes of self-dehumanizing. Because the fantasist gains some sense of sharing existence with the other-than-human, the fantasist arrives at a formal position analogous to that of the *Beowulf* poet, who dwells where strange creatures are natural, even though they may be hateful to man and god. Because the science fiction writer, like the fantasist, starts from an enchantment-deprived condition, by extrapolation he cannot arrive at significant otherness, for in the modern world there is nothing that matters but rationalized humanity and its products. Extrapolation can lead only to revelation of more extreme effects of human success, the ultimate being humanity's self-destruction.

The paradox that our progress can dehumanize us may be clarified by an analogy with biologists' explanation of extreme variations in species' populations. One form of caterpillar, say, begins to flourish. Its numbers expand each year and it increasingly overwhelms competing organisms, until, finally, a particular environment is dominated by this one kind of caterpillar. The result is rapid exhaustion of food supply and desperate intraspecies struggles. Climactic growth of numbers is followed by a quick collapse that diminishes the population below its original normal level. Cultural dehumanization, of course, is neither so mechanical nor so purely a material process, but that it is subtler in its operation makes it no less dangerous. What is perhaps most pernicious about technological progress is that it brings indubitable intellectual as well as physical benefits, so that literary responses to it are driven into paradoxical modes, such as the subversive oxymoron of fantasy.

That progress may all too effectively dehumanize us must be seen as a fundamental problematic at the heart of science fiction's extrapolations. The genre's sustaining paradox is that its aliens are not really strange. They are, most commonly, disguised human beings of different times, places, or metaphysical persuasions. These false aliens are, at best, foreigners, not others: "rather than a confrontation with a radical other . . . we have to do with an outsider constituted as such within a specific historical situation."[17] By time or space travel we are carried away from the earthly otherness of fantasy, for the creatures of fantasy are not foreigners; they are native, however alien to humans. The dragon in *Beowulf*, for example, has lived in Beowulf's kingdom longer than the hero.

THE FUTURE OF *THE TIME MACHINE*

My distinction between science fiction and fantasy exalts neither at the expense of the other. The forms embody two responses to the same historical circumstance, humankind's domination of the natural world so completely that it becomes difficult to conceive of beings other than humans, or of nonhuman modes of existence, or even to imagine what might be termed "magic," in the sense of occurrences not answerable to humankind's rational analyses and naturalistic explanations. So it is not surprising that science fiction has become the more popular and often attempted genre in our century. Of this trend the most spectacular settings of *Frankenstein* are prophetic—the highest Alps, the remotest Hebrides, and arctic wastelands: even by 1818 there was very little unhumanized space left on the globe. And the pace has accelerated. The original film *King Kong* of the early thirties presented Kong as a danger, but in the remake of the early 1970s he appears as an endangered species to be protected. And Kong's transformation into something like an oversized snail darter calls attention to the importance of the life sciences to science fiction, as is apparent already in *Frankenstein*, which also displays a bias toward the kind of technology favored by science fiction. But both of these features are even more vividly illustrated in H. G. Wells's first "scientific romance," commonly treated as paradigmatic of the genre in the twentieth century, *The Time Machine*.[18]

Wells's title says it all. Science fiction does not require much gadgetry, yet the genre can flourish only in a technological civilization, for the machine is the preeminent manifestation of humankind's capacity for dehumanizing itself. And processes of mechanical reproduction are always important to the genre—Frankenstein could have made another monster, and very nearly did. The making of one time machine implies the possibility of others, even, perhaps, mass production and finally inexpensive Japanese models. So, too, the seemingly unique adventure of a typical science fiction story possesses a peculiar quality: it, or something very much like it, could happen to someone else. A second time traveler who reached the year 802,701 would face essentially the same situation with Eloi and Morlocks as Wells's original traveler. This repeatable quality is not a defect but a sign of the genre's adherence to realism, as our scientific society defines reality. Without a potential of reiterability the experience of a distant place or time could not to a scientific mind seem entirely authentic.[19] Extrapolation of scientific attitudes implies emphasis on replicability, and the work of art of an age of mechanical reproduction appropriately diminishes the importance of uniqueness. In this regard, science fiction is the opposite of myth, myth being timeless because it represents the beginning of time; in myth, a unique event establishes a future pattern.

The replicable and unmythic character of science fiction is interestingly suggested by the most poetic touch in *The Time Machine*, the flowers the traveler inadvertently brings back in his pocket, whose origin could well be a speculation of Coleridge's, "If a man could pass through Paradise in a dream, and have a flower presented to him as a pledge that his soul had really been there, and if he found the flower in his hand when he awoke—Aye! and what then?" But the year 802,701 is, unmistakably, not paradise, so that the poignance of Wells's flowers lies in their suggestion of a possibility of return, whereas Coleridge's flower reminds us of the mystery of the gulf separating fallen man and lost divinity. We are asked to imagine Wells's flowers as real, meaning testable by scientific means, as in the story it is suggested that they be so scientifically tested. Coleridge's flower is other, something belonging nowhere in our botany.

Time is as important to science fiction as the machine, and Wells's romance makes it plain that it is essentially Darwinian time on which the genre depends.[20] *The Time Machine* is a brilliant imagining of a course of evolution on earth given the scientifically understood nature of our solar system. Hence the story's most compelling episode is not the main one involving the Eloi and Morlocks but the brief trip beyond to the cooling globe where all but the most elementary life forms have perished. This apparently unfunctional passage (originally added by Wells at an editor's request) powerfully seizes the imagination because it portrays the inevitable end of earthly life as biological and geological sciences must extrapolate it.[21] Without denying the influence on Wells of the depressing second law of thermodynamics, I would suggest that his principal orientation is determined by his recognizing that the scientific imagination, because it is scientific, is obligated to rigorous following through of a particular sequence of causes and effects to their farthest foreseeable consequences, however unpleasant these may be. Entropy aside, the true darkness implicit in evolutionary thinking is not that it implies humankind emerged from lower organisms, but that it must postulate man's transiency. Evolutionary thinking is frightening because it expands our capacity to imagine our inevitable natural doom. Only man, it has often been observed, imagines his death. Perhaps only modern man has been able fully and exactly to imagine the natural extinction of his species. It is this awful power that science fiction taps.

Revealing of how deeply Darwinianism enters into Wells's art is his fine though little-known story, "Æpyornis Island," first published in 1894 (see Appendix 1). The story, out of print for more than seventy-five years, not only points up Wells's fascination with zoology but his shrewd insight into the commercialization of scientific collecting empowered by Darwinian ideas. That commercialization serves, furthermore, to focus attention on the apparent paradox of the modern western European's brutal contempt for primitive people manifesting itself in a scientific endeavor to preserve fossil evidence of earlier forms of life. Few brief stories illustrate so vividly the savage paradoxes of progress that are the secret springs of science fiction, while providing so cogent a stylistic contrast of the genre's realism with self-involuting intricacy of the best fantasy writing, manifested, for instance, in García Márquez's "The Last Voyage of the Ghost Ship."

The Time Machine, however, displays more poignantly how germane to science fiction is *Frankenstein's* representation of the impossibility of our ceasing to use our imaginations, even when so imagining tends to our distress rather than satisfaction. And the genre is best understood as literature focused on why science is now our fate, because science is our most systematized effort to realize the unique capabilities (for good or ill) of humankind. What the modern age must face more directly than any earlier epoch is the threatening pressure exerted on us by our very gift for conceiving future possibilities.

Wells's novel proves that Victor Frankenstein's inconsistency foretells our own. Condemning scientific accomplishment on the ground of its catastrophic results one moment, the next Victor endorses scientific aspiration:

> Seek happiness in tranquility and avoid ambition, even if it be only the apparently innocent one of distinguishing yourself in science and discoveries. Yet why do I say this? I have myself been blasted in these hopes, yet another may succeed. (206)

Nuclear destruction appears our likely destiny today, yet how many blame Einstein for writing to Roosevelt the letter that started us along this road? If we would condemn Victor Frankenstein, as I believe we should, we must recognize that in so doing we condemn ourselves—and some such critique, I believe, lurks in the depth of the best science fiction.

With the development of modern scientific thought, imagination was liberated to explore the future. It is only with the emergence of evolutionary theory in the nineteenth century, however, that this mode of imagining could reach fulfillment. Only then could a literary genre thoroughly engaged with rational conceptions of our species' destiny elaborates itself. This is why virtually all the best science fiction is, explicitly or implicitly, a kind of time travel, an exploration into possible significancies of living beings functioning in a transformatively developmental fashion. Both the individual and groups of individuals are represented in a perspective of species evolution, which, as in Wells's *Time Machine*, may of course become devolution. Most works in this genre focus on a projected future,

or on the collocation of individuals or groups at diverse evolutionary stages, these defined either in directly biological terms or
with cultural stages superimposed. And because science fiction is
thus a post-Darwinian genre, its affiliations with earlier literary
forms are at best tenuous. Earlier travelers to the moon, or
shrewd visitors from exotic lands certainly encountered cultural
differences, but never were these represented as involved with
evolutionary processes. Whatever *Beowulf*'s dragon may be, it
does not in the Anglo-Saxon poem appear as a primitive life
form. Science fiction, significantly, begins to flourish when the
concept of the primitive emerges as a potent intellectual force, at
the end of the nineteenth century—an event, as I observe later,
destructive to fantasy.

PLAIN STYLE AND
DEPERSONALIZED CHARACTERIZATION

Science fiction's evolutionary tendency, along with its bias toward the repeatable and away from the unique, helps to explain
why the genre, as shrewder critics have pointed out, so seldom
develops individual characterizations.[22] Technological development may seem to make the individual independent of social
needs. But in a technological society, in fact, differentiation of
individuals is of negative value. A computer, for instance, works
best if its operators all behave in the same way. Science fiction is
perhaps the literary form that most vividly reflects the increasing
devaluation of individuality and resistance to social arrangements
founded on respect for heterogeneity. Wells's time traveler, like
Frankenstein's monster, is, prophetically, nameless. This feature
deserves attention, if only because the narrative form of science
fiction owes much to realistic prose fiction, the genre that
throughout the eighteenth and nineteenth centuries abounded
in richly individualized characterizations. But exactly what is
most scientific in science fiction is its exploitation of the impersonal discourse favored by scientists. Science fiction goes beyond
realistic fiction in that it may with perfect propriety address us
solely in the nonmetaphoric, unselfconscious, simply referential
prose that has been the preferred language of science since the

founding of the Royal Society. This aggressively plain style contributed much, as scholars like Ian Watt have shown, to the growth of realistic fiction, but in a work such as *The Time Machine* the style of expository realism gains special thematic significance. The substantive wonders of the story must be represented in a manner which will transform their remarkableness into probability. A genre that extrapolates can only be thus cooly sensational. In this form we are not to be lost in wonder or enchanted by marvels, least of all those arising from the very texture of verbal representation.

There is no inherent restraint on ordinary novelists in the language they use, or in the narrative structures they may employ, so novelists have regularly experimented, innovated, and developed increasingly reflexive stylistic modes. But science fiction is committed to linguistic and structural conservatism. If it becomes adventurous in manner it endangers its scientific standing. It cannot be hospitable to writers exhuberantly adventurous with language, a Charles Dickens, a Henry James, or a James Joyce. Science fiction cannot easily incline toward making its own artistry its principal subject. This stylistic and formal limitation is connected to the genre's thematic conservatism. Many think of the genre as speculatively future-oriented, but much of it duplicitously presents us with pictures of the past as if they were images of the future. H. G. Wells, in fact, is unusual in the intensity with which he imagines future evolutionary processes. It is more common to find that the fastest spaceships carry us to the farthest galaxies to enjoy visions of past history— sword-play, hunting-and-gathering social groups, natural medicine, and so forth. This presentation of the human past disguised as a future or faraway life is symptomatic of a more important feature: science fiction's reluctance to look inward. It is not a self-questioning, self-challenging genre. Inwardness, self-reflexivity, and the exploration of self-recursive modes are the characteristics of fantasy. Fantasy responds to the modern conditions of rationalized civilization, culture deprived of enchantment, by seeking to uncover magic possibilities, especially in the processes of linguistic articulation and narrative in themselves. To put the distinction perhaps too simply yet with a clarity necessary to effective criticism, fantasy is self-fantasticating as science fiction is not. To cast a spell, fantasy must be a spell, the texture of its enunciation must be magical, in the sense of bringing forward the amazingly transformative, because self-transformative, powers of language, exactly what science, and so science fiction, seeks to exorcise.

CHAPTER THREE

Doubt That Is Not Denial

No man would find an abiding strangeness on the Moon
unless he were the sort of man who could find it in his own
back garden.

C. S. LEWIS, *Of Other Worlds*

OMANTIC FANTASY DEVELOPED SELF-REFLEXIVELY
the intense skepticism fostered by enlight-
ened rationality, seeking not to dismiss or
ignore the power that had destroyed superstition but to redirect systematized disbelief
against itself. If such a purpose seems remote
and esoteric, one may consider it as not
unlike Michael Polanyi's concern for the tacit dimension of
human experience, a concern provoked by a conversation with
Bukharin, a leading Soviet theoretician under Stalin. Burkharin
told Polanyi that "pure science was a morbid symptom of a class
society" and that in Russia "the conception of science pur-
sued for its own sake would disappear." Polanyi was struck, he
reports,

> that this denial of the very existence of independent
> scientific thought came from a social theory which
> derived its tremendous persuasive power from its claim
> to scientific certainty. The scientific outlook appeared to
> have produced a mechanic conception of man and
> history in which there was no place for science itself.
> This conception denied altogether any intrinsic power
> for thought and thus denied also any grounds for
> claiming freedom of thought.[1]

31

Polanyi's attack on what he calls "skeptical fanaticism" has distant intellectual roots in Romanticism, but Romantics such as Keats were on principle less self-assured than the modern scientist-philosopher. They dramatized only the wisdom of welcoming the pleasures and anxieties of living without absolute certainties, even of questioning that there could be any such certainties, thus fostering what Keats called "negative capability." This view required that the *form* of their literary fantasies be self-challenging and therefore lacking in the confident assertiveness and reliability not merely of scientific analysis but also of the major traditional literary genres. It is not surprising then, that fantasy has been rarer in recent literature than science fiction, and also that in the Romantic era itself the function of fantasy was necessarily a highly problematic one even for those who wrote it.

SUPERNATURAL AND ORDINARY

The finest fantasies of British Romanticism, Coleridge's "The Rime of the Ancient Mariner" and Keats's "La Belle Dame Sans Merci," for example, are literary ballads that seem to stand somewhat apart from the principal literary accomplishments of their epoch. Why this should be so is suggested by Coleridge when he describes the origin of *Lyrical Ballads* in the 1798 edition of which "The Ancient Mariner" was the first poem. Coleridge contrasts his purposes and Wordsworth's in terms that have seemed to some a shade defensive, as if the junior partner in the joint enterprise was aware that his contribution was of a secondary character.

> The thought suggested itself . . . that a series of poems might be composed of two sorts. In the one, the incidents and agents were to be, in part at least, supernatural; and the excellence aimed at was to consist in the interesting of the affections by the dramatic truth of such emotions, as would naturally accompany such situations, supposing them real. And real in *this* sense they have been to every human being who, from what

ever source of delusion, has at any time believed himself under supernatural agency. For the second class, subjects were to be chosen from ordinary life; . . .

. . . [m]y endeavors should be directed to persons and characters supernatural, or at least romantic; yet so as to transfer from our inward nature a human interest and a semblance of truth sufficient to procure for these shadows of imagination that willing suspension of disbelief for the moment, which constitutes poetic faith. Mr. Wordsworth . . . was . . . to give the charm of novelty to things of every day, and to excite a feeling analogous to the supernatural, by awakening the mind's attention from the lethargy of custom, and directing it to the loveliness and the wonders of the world before us.[2]

The ground of Coleridge's contrast of the supernatural to the ordinary, subjects romantic to everyday subjects, the parallel that makes discrimination possible, is that the supernatural may be believed (even if that belief is mistaken), and that appropriate treatment of the commonplace and everyday will "excite a feeling analogous to the supernatural." This strikes me as rather undefensive, because the efficacy of poetry of the everyday is judged by its success in evoking feelings like those of supernatural experience. Wordsworth's task, directing the readers' minds to "the wonders of the world before us," implies that nonfantastic Romantic poetry will by defamiliarizing arouse a marveling response. But in reacting against the Enlightenment's mechanistic rationalism, Wordsworth and Coleridge inevitably found themselves resisting the onset of modern mass, urbanized technological culture when they strove to affirm the preciousness of ordinary experience.[3] To this effort to improve the conditions of normal contemporary thinking and feeling, fantasy might seem to have little to contribute. Despite what some handbooks assert, moreover, Romantics were seldom nostalgic about the past. Their attempt to recover features of earlier ways of life being lost in modern society's rush to progress was intended to enhance the consciousness and sensibility of contemporary readers. The wonder provoked by fantasy, therefore, was a relatively rare alternative to wonder attained through defamiliarizing. Nonetheless, fantasies were not outside the mainstream of Romantic literary aspirations, even though Coleridge's admission that fantasies must somehow redirect skepticism ("disbelief") alerts us that the intricacy of their form will surpass that of more naturalistic narratives.

Such complexity is signaled by an important formal similarity between "The Ancient Mariner" and "La Belle Dame." Coleridge's "It is an Ancient Mariner / And he stoppeth one of three," is reflected by Keats's ballad's beginning with the question, "What can ail thee, Knight at arms?" We come upon both Mariner and Knight as unanticipated figures, who *respond* to startled questions by the Wedding Guest and Keats's narrator: both poems are dialogic in character. Because they are dialogic, in neither does the narrator's mere credibility become a major issue. I find no critics who doubt that the Mariner and the Knight believe that they are telling the truth. And one tends to believe in their belief (however mistaken one may judge it to be) just because their tales are so fantastic. This paradox carries us to the core of Romantic fantasy, which always includes a questioning of the possibility of fantasy in our skeptical, rationalistic, disenchanted modern world. Such questioning forestalls the danger of delusionary self-enthrallment, for example, self-victimizing by nostalgia.

Romantic fantasy, as Coleridge's statement in the *Biographica Literaria* implies, is about renewing possibilities of impossible fantasy, bringing before us magical events in full awareness that magic is no longer credible. So fantasy poses a peculiar problem for critical analysis. To define fantasy's meaning by explaining or justifying its impossibilities is to lose contact (as Tolkien asserted) with both how and why it comes into existence. Criticism must somehow deal with an artistic experience of confronting as real what one knows cannot be real, the arousal of belief in the unbelievable, for this is the underlying oxymoron of discourse distinguishing Romantic fantasy as a literary form.

Another quality of Romantic fantasy disabling for criticism is illuminated by a second parallel between "The Ancient Mariner" and "La Belle Dame." Both finally abandon the reader in a state of uncertainty; "willing suspension of disbelief" means leaving the reader suspended. One is unsure even as to how conclusive the stories-within-stories may be, just as when the events recounted may have occurred is left significantly indeterminate. The Mariner passes on to exercise elsewhere on others his strange power of speech, and the destiny of Keats's Knight, however well or ill he has accounted for his sojourning, remains undefined. Both poems narrate experiences intrinsically coherent but lacking full closure. Romantic fantasy is a transient as well as an interruptive mode, and any explanation of the fashion in which it functions outside regular structures of causality, that does away with its eruptive and definitively inconclusive quality, falsifies it.[4]

The refusal of fantasy to cohere with ordinary systems of order, so that in the very mode of its telling it casts doubt on the meaning of what it tells, however rigorous the structure of its telling may be, may have been part of what Coleridge referred to when, according to his nephew, he observed to Mrs. Barbauld that "The Ancient Mariner" had too much moral.

> It ought to have had no more moral than the *Arabian Nights'* tale of the merchant's sitting down to eat dates by the side of a well, and throwing the shells aside, and lo! a genie starts up, and say he *must* kill the aforesaid merchant, *because* one of the date shells had, it seems, put out the eye of the genie's son.[5]

A crux in this comment is the genie's invocation of the familiar law of cause and effect: the merchant is victimized by the sheerly accidental conjunction of two modes of existence so alien that one is invisible to the other. One implication of Coleridge's story is that a willing suspension of disbelief may profit you nothing by any normal system of accounting, which is why most explanations of fantasy work hard to explain it away. Objectors to Robert Penn Warren's celebrated interpretation of "The Ancient Mariner" accuse Warren of reducing the poem to a structure founded on traditional Christian belief that eliminates what intrigues and baffles us in the poem, namely, its fantastic quality dependent on the appearance of an order—not mere disorder—incongruent with our conventional conceptions of how reality functions. Fantasy as fantasy cannot satisfy those seeking purely rational rewards of critical exegesis, because it arises from an event evanescent and unnecessary even if—or because—manifesting some alien system. The fantastic experience must delight or grieve us *because* it is in normal terms unfunctional, unexpectable, and unrepeatable. It is to be treasured, in joy or sorrow, because truly gratuitous.

WORDSWORTH THE INSPIRER OF "LA BELLE DAME"?

There is no essence of Romantic fantasy which permits us to formulate useful general definitions of it. We can even say little about how it comes into being. Here "La Belle Dame" is peculiarly illustrative, for how Keats came to write the poem remains a mystery that has troubled several commentators, especially since he seems neither before nor after to have attempted anything quite like it, and his own opinion of the poem continues to be a subject for controversy.

"La Belle Dame Sans Merci" was probably written on April 21, 1819, possibly a week later, just before the composition of the series of great odes during May 1819, poems on which much of Keats's fame is founded.[6] The most valuable piece of the scanty evidence as to what might have inspired Keats to write the ballad is provided by the long journal letter to his brother and sister-in-law in which the first version of the poem was inserted. Keats's humorously casual manner and his readiness to record with seeming spontaneity whatever occurs to him at each moment of writing, however, makes the testimony of the journal-letter entries difficult to assess. On April 15, for example, he writes with fervor of his increasing pleasure in the fifth canto of *The Divine Comedy*, and includes a sonnet inspired by Dante's work, "As Hermes once," which in theme and some details has understandably been regarded as anticipating "La Belle Dame." Yet the sonnet is followed immediately by merry bandinage, "Are there any flowers in bloom you like . . . any streets full of Corset makers?" (Rollins, 92).

In the entries just preceding April 21, however, some details recur that point toward themes occurring in the ballad. There is, for instance, Keats's unhappiness about the "cruel deception" involved in the letters between his now deceased brother Tom and "Amenia," a fictitious woman supposedly in love with Tom, an invention of one C. J. Wells, who forged, "Amenia's" letters. And Keats reports meeting Coleridge, who treated him to a monologue that began with nightingales and poetry, proceeded through analyses of different kinds of dreams with comments on monsters, and concluded with a ghost story. But most consistently on Keats's mind during these days is his friend Reynolds' forthcoming parody of Wordsworth's soon-to-be published ballad "Peter Bell." While it is doubtless reductive to read the spoofing couplets of "When they will come into Faery's court" that Keats inserted into his letter as merely allegorical of Wordsworth, Coleridge, and Keats himself, the lines do contain at least one echo of *The White Doe of Rylestone*, and there seems little doubt that in mid-April Keats's mind kept coming back to Wordsworth.

On April 20 Keats comments on his review for *The Examiner* of Reynolds' parody. Taking off from Reynolds' epigraph, "I am the real Simon Pure," Keats sets up a contrast between a "false florimel" and a "pamphleteering Archimage" (thus calling attention to passages in Spenser most often cited as sources for his ballad) as a means for maneuvering, in the words he used to his brother and sister-in-law, "To keep clear of all parties" (Rollins, 93–94). Although Reynolds has written parody, Keats claims his friend has "sympathetically felt the finer parts of Mr. Wordsworth's poetry." And Keats concludes, "If we are one part pleased at this, we are three parts sorry that an appreciator of Wordsworth should show so much temper at the really provoking name of Peter Bell." (Rollins, 94). The sentence sums up the ambivalent complexity with which Keats himself responded to Wordsworth's poetry. In the present instance, it seems a fair guess that Keats was especially provoked by the older poet's use of balladic form for thoroughly, even aggressively, naturalistic purposes. It is worth noting that both "Peter Bell" and "The Idiot Boy," (the practical target of Reynolds' parody and, as a kind of anti-"Ancient Mariner," a fine focus for Wordsworth's antisupernaturalist role in *Lyrical Ballads*), demonstrate the wonder of what is purely natural. Both are, in fact, powerful demonstrations of the irrelevance of supernaturalism and Wordsworth's ambitions to defamiliarize rather than fantasize. This could not but irritate Keats because he was so sympathetic to Wordsworth's appeal to the wonder of the commonplace. Keats was strongly drawn to Wordsworth's faith that the primary task for poets of their time was to strip away a veil of familiarity from the beauty and power of actual daily experience. And Keats found congenial Wordsworth's contempt for sentimental falsifiers of humble and simple life. But it seems certain that Keats wished also to defend his delight in Spenserian Florimels; he did not want poetry reduced to little more than "really provoking" Peter Bells. So it is possible to suspect that Reynolds' parody of Wordsworth may have goaded him toward trying to create a more authentically anti-Wordsworthian, if necessarily deeply ambiguous, supernaturalism such as we find in "La Belle Dame."

In suggesting that Keats, like Coleridge before him, though less programmatically, fantasized in opposition to Wordsworthian practice, I imply that in so doing he engaged in a struggle with the ideal of naturalism which flourished at the end of the eighteenth century. To summarize in grotesquely reductive fashion the central difficulty in this complicated issue: the naturalistic ideal of a direct and more-or-less transparent rendering of appearances excludes a dynamic complexity intrinsic to *any* act of artistic creation. To make a poem is to employ cultural skills to shape a representation of natural phenomena which the poem, as a cultural artifact, surpasses—at the risk, of course, of losing contact with external reality. This is why *all* significant poems can be said to involve some *supranatural* aspects (as cultural artifacts they go beyond the purely natural), and why a poem in any way committed to truth to nature will falsify itself through the mere fact of representing the natural in cultural terms. Just as Romantic fantasy sought not to do away with skeptical rationalism but to apply it to its own functioning, so Romantic fantasy sought not to deny all the values of naturalistic ideals of art (of which Wordsworth was a powerful practitioner) but to articulate the inherent limits in that admirable ideal. Of course Keats's feelings toward Wordsworth on this matter, as on

others, had to be ambivalent, for he sought not to deny the value
of what Wordsworth had accomplished but only to doubt that his
art, or any art, could be or should be regarded as the only valid
kind of poetry.

Observing that his review of Reynolds' parody is "a little
politic," Keats concludes the report of his article with a self-
justification that foretells ambiguities essential to the success of
his ballad: "I believe what I say nay I am sure I do—I and my
conscience are in luck today—which is an excellent thing" (Rollins, 94). Keats here seems moving unmistakably in the direction
of Coleridge's comments on suspended disbelief and the reality of
some people's belief in supernaturalism, at least at some times. A
Romantic poet undertaking fantasy of necessity must put himself
in a state of mind in which he can believe he thinks what he says.
In a disenchanted world, he must enchant himself. So perhaps it
is not surprising that Keats so suddenly inserts "La Belle Dame"
into his letter, and follows it by an often-quoted joking paragraph
about four kisses rather than twenty. But it is worth citing both
Keats's first version of the poems presented by Rollins, since
problems of versions will come upon us very soon, and appending his following comment, that reveals (in my view) not so
much unease as a liberated sense of self-mockery quite in accord
with the self-quizzical assurance of "I believe I think what I say."

> La belle dame sans merci—
> O what can ail thee knight at a[r]ms
>   Alone and palely loitering?
> The sedge has withered from the Lake
>   And no birds sing!
>
> O What can ail thee knight at a[r]ms
>   So haggard and so woe begone?
> The squirrel's granary is full
>   And the harvest's done.
>
> I see {a} lily on thy brow   {death's}
>   With anguish moist and fever dew,
> And on thy cheeks {a} fading rose   {death's}
>   Fast Withereth too—

I met a Lady in the {Meads} {Wilds}
  Full beautiful, a faery's child
Her hair was long, her foot was light
  And her eyes were wild—

I made a Garland for her head,
  And bracelets too, and fragrant Zone{s}
She look'd at me as she'd did love
  And made sweet moan—

I set her on my pacing steed
  And nothing else saw all day long
For sidelong would she bend and sing
  A faerys song—

She found me roots of relish sweet
  And honey wild and {honey} dew {manna}
And sure in language strange she said
  I love thee true—

She took me to her elfin grot {and sig'd full sore}
  And there she wept {and there she sighed full
  sore}
And there I shut her wild wild eyes
  With kisses four.

And there she lulled me asleep
  And there I drean'd Ah Woe betide!
The latest dream I ever dreamt
  On the cold hill side

I saw pale kings and Princes too
  Pale warriors death pale were they all
They cried La belle dame sans merci
  Thee hath in thrall.

> I saw their starv'd lips in the gloam
> {All tremble}   gaped
> With {horrid} warning ^ wide   {agape}
> And I awoke and found me here
> On the cold hill's side
>
> And this is way I {wither} sojurn here
> Alone and palely loitering;
> Though the sedge is wither'd frome the Lak{e}
> And no birds sing—. . . . .

Why four kisses— you will say—why four because I wish to restrain the headlong impetuosity of my Muse— she would have fain said 'score' without hurting the rhyme—but we must temper the Imagination as the Critics say with Judgment. I was obliged to choose an even number that both eyes might have fair play: and to speak truly I think two a piece quite sufficient—Suppose I had said seven; there would have been three and a half a piece—a very awkward affair—and well got out of on my side—

(Rollins, 95–97; words in braces outside the stanzas were crossed out by Keats, replaced by the words in braces in the stanzas; brackets enclose Rollins emendations of omitted letters.)

Paradoxical as it may at first seem, Keats's capacity for humorous self-criticism helps to make the creation of his ballad possible, just as Coleridge's willing suspension of disbelief implies that skeptical intelligence will be active in the creation of a dramatic truth about superstitious feelings. Fantasy was not, and could not be, for a Romantic poet something simply and casually spontaneous, even though it might be unexpected and unnecessary. It could not be detached from a quizzical, if unanxious, self-consciousness about such an undertaking. Romantic fantasy, after all, offers itself to interpretive communities in which magic, enchantment, and active faith in supernaturalism are no longer tolerated.

Many contemporary commentators postulate a mind-set necessary for both the creation and sympathetic reception of fantasy close to negative capability, a capacity to be " "in uncertainties, Mysteries, doubts, without any irritable reaching after fact & reason" (Rollins, 1, 193–94). The hesitancy Todorov identifies as essential to the experience of the fantastic plainly is close to what Keats describes, although Todorov can't conceive of one wishing to persist in such a condition. An even more illuminating parallel with difference appears in the remarks of Rosemary Jackson, who is drawn to emphasize the negativity of fantastic literature. But, unlike Keats, she conceives of this negativity less as openness and receptivity than as a specific antagonism to predominant conceptions of reality. The fantastic, she says,

> introduces areas which can be conceptualized only by negative terms according to the categories of nineteenth-century realism: thus, the im-possible, the unreal, the nameless, formless, shapeless, un-known, invisible. What could be termed a "bourgeois" category of the real is under attack. It is this *negative relationality* which constitutes the meaning of the modern fantastic.[7]

Jackson calls our attention to an important truth, that Romantic fantasy does indeed resist too limiting definitions of reality, or, perhaps more precisely, responds to contradictions in the concept of the natural. But Jackson lacks Keatsian skepticism even about skepticism which undergirds his negative capability, so that in contrast to a devout Marxist like her, he is even willing to entertain the possibility of supernatural occurrences, and is content simply to hover "upon the confines of truth."

To put the matter as simply as possible: most of the charm of "La Belle Dame" lies in the strangeness of its meaning, not only its intrinsic uncertainties but also the indeterminacy of its relation to anything in the world of our normal experience, including other poems by John Keats. Such openness would be constricted by too anxious a demand for authoritatively systematic connection of poem to context, and Keats's humorous remarks about his ballad may be read not merely as evidence that he was not naively enthralled by his own magic but also as an attempt to protect its unconnectedness, what might be called the gratuitousness of its inspiration.

That Keats's praise for an ability to accept the irresolvability of certain doubts and unconnectability of certain situations was not a personal peculiarity but characteristic of other Romantics as well, is suggested by Charles Lamb's objection to what he called the Caledonian character in "Imperfect Sympathies." Lamb scornfully describes a character the reverse of the negatively capable:

> You never witness his first apprehension of a thing. His understanding is always at its meridian—you never see the first dawn, the early streaks.—He has no falterings of self-suspicion. Surmises, guesses, misgivings, half-intuitions, semi-consciousness, partial illuminations, dim instincts, embryo conceptions, have not place in his brain, or vocabulary. . . . Between the affirmative and the negative there is no border-land with him. You cannot hover with him upon the confines of truth.[8]

For Keats, Reynolds in his parody is too simply antagonistic to Wordsworth, because Keats wishes to resist the older poet only so far as he would seem to deny the virtues of a less drastically naturalistic, let us say, a Spenserian or Dantean art. Yet Keats, who could so keenly appreciate both the hatefulness of a quarrel in the street and the fineness of the energies therein displayed, was inevitably sympathetic to Wordworth's insistence that a true poetic response would never involve a turning away from the low or coarse or common. Keats resisted Wordsworth on the basis of Wordsworthian principle: a good poet will reject any kind of exclusivity. Keat's objection to "Peter Bell" centers on its implicit reverse snobbism, which would denigrate the fantastic and the magical.

WHICH BELLE DAME?

There is good reason for Keats to have been ambivalent about fantasy and to have written little of it, and it is not surprising that he could be flippant about his ballad, so fervently admired by so many subsequent critics, nor that he did not choose to republish the poem in his 1820 *Lamia* volume. That choice, however, makes it impossible to determine which version of "La Belle Dame" Keats preferred, this textual uncertainty raising a host of problems for critics as well as editors. The first scholar fully to survey these issues was Francis Lee Utley, who a quarter of a century ago brought to bear on the problem extensive knowledge of folklore as well as literature. More recently, Jerome J. McGann has readdressed the textual problem as part of his concern with principles of editing.[9] After writing "La Belle Dame" in his letter of April 1819, Keats did nothing with the poem until he published it in Leigh Hunt's *Indicator* in May 1820, signing it "Caviare," and introducing a few but some quite significant changes from the version in his letter of the previous year. Ordinarily the *Indicator* text would be the basis for printing the poem in standard editions of Keats's work, but, instead, the text appearing in Richard Monckton Miles' *Life, Letters, and Literary Remains of John Keats* (1848) has more frequently been used. This version is based on a copy made by Charles Brown, though what exactly he copied is unknown. McGann asserts that the Brown version has been favored by editors because it is more overtly romantic than the *Indicator* version, which, notably through its use of "wight" rather than "Knight at arms," sets up ironic overtones, alerting its readers that the poet is self-consciously exploiting an archaic form and subtly urging them to respond skeptically to the poem's subject matter—an attitude reinforced by the signature "Caviare," calling to mind Hamlet's "caviare to the general." Though I find McGann's argument persuasive, a majority of critics and editors, notably Jack Stillinger, have chosen the Brown version over the *Indicator* one on asthetic grounds, some citing the change in the latter as indicative of Keat's incompetence at revising his verse—Earl Wasserman in a famous reading ignores the possibility of seriously considering the *Indicator* text.[10]

McGann's polemics on editorial practice and theory oversimplify and thereby diminish the intensity of the critical difficulties posed by the poem's versions, difficulties that have led some very good editors, Douglas Bush and Miriam Allott, for example, to print both versions. The crux of the matter is focused by Wasserman's objection to the *Indicator* version simply as poor revising, for the Brown version has attracted praise in part because it is closer to the original text appearing in the letter of April 1819. In the Brown version, as in the letter, the protagonist is a Knight, not a wight, and the lady lulls him to sleep, rather than, as in the *Indicator* text, their falling asleep together after a mutual exchange of kisses. (Both the Brown version and the *Indicator* text will be found at the end of note 10, on pages 169–72, below.)

Utley's analysis of such differences was the first carefully extensive one, and it remains one of the most thorough and judicious, directing critical evaluation toward the significance of the increase in the number and kinds of uncertainty introduced by Keats's changes. The transforming of "knight" to "wight," for example, probably reflects the influence of Keats's reading of Spenser, but, one must ask, in what did that influence consist? The question is difficult even to raise seriously today, because Spenser is far out of favor, and even for Keats some aspects of Spenser's art, such as his moral allegory, appear to have had little attraction. If we assume that Keats was most drawn to Spenser's language and imagery, we may find it possible that he noticed how Spenser's "wight" normally means simply a human being, not necessarily a good or a bad person, not one confined to a special stratum of society, and applicable to both men and women. Spenser's "wight" is a rather unexclusive term, wheras knight refers to a masculine figure and carries connotations of both power and definite social status. The change, therefore, from "Knight at arms" to "wretched wight" redirects a reader's perception of the poem's protagonist, bringing him closer to Coleridge's anonymous Mariner. There is certainly a difference in how one responds to the strange experience recounted by the protagonist depending on whether one imagines him as armored knight or wretched wight. And in stanza ten, in which the protagonist dreams of kings, princes, and warriors, the relations of these to a knight would be different from those to an ordinary person—although, of course, a wight *might* be a knight, for Spenser often calls knights wights.

It is worth observing, moreover, that what the pale kings, princes, and warriors tell the dreamer reveals little more than what we are told by the title of the poem, whose ambiguity is exemplified by Michael Flanders' spoofing translation of it: "The Beautiful Lady Who Never Says Thank You." More important than the dubiety of individual words, however, is the fashion in which the deepest recessiveness of the poem's inset dialogues, the inquirer-narrator reporting the protagonist's account of the warning from figures of whom he dreamed, rather than clarifying anything or advancing our understanding, returns us to the poem's title. The ballad does not explain the title, nor the title the ballad.

The poem thus might be said to catch up the reader in an experience as weird as that of the protagonist, whose final answer to the question that provoked his story simply sends us back into his story. In his phrase "And this is why I sojourn here," the antecedent to "this" appears to be the whole tale he has just told, so the interpreting reader is returned through the story that presents more problems than solutions to the original query: why?

In the *Indicator* version the protagonist, in recounting what brought him to this place and current condition, moreover, emphasizes that he first entangled the belle dame with garland, bracelet, and zone, before putting her on his horse, so that she at first appears to be his captive. Thereafter she gradually takes the initiative, finding exotic food and taking him to her grot. But the speaker's transformation from dominant figure to thrall is complicated by Keats's revising, which changes "there she lulled me asleep" to "there we slumbered." Indeed, the revision, with "I shut her wild, sad eyes / So kissed to sleep" implies she slumbered first—the exact reverse of "she lulled me asleep." If, like Wasserman, one chiefly values the poem's rational sequentiality, Keats's changes will be unattractive. But the increased complexity of the later version may be regarded as a deepening of the dubieties fundamental to the poem's strange "charm" from the very first, such as the uncertainty in the phrasing, "as she did love," and the oxymoron of "sweet moan."

Unquestionably Keats's revision increases contradictions disrupting the relatively simple presentation of the original in which the knight appears victimized by demonic lady. But even the original is tinged with dictional and thematic uncertainties: "as she did love" (meaning she really didn't?) and the unsureness implicit "*sure* in language strange." So tiny a shift in the penultimate stanza of "gloam" to "gloom" may be seen as blurring the clarity of knight victimized. "Gloam" refers principally to the natural transition of day to evening, here perhaps imaging the speaker's physical situation when he speaks, in autumn, between the abundance of summer and the desolation of winter. The change to "gloom" would seem to emphasize the speaker's view, the darkness of his vision as opposed to the objective circumstances in which he speaks, thereby accentuating for the reader the possible inaccuracy or bias in his account of what occurred.

"WALKING IN MYSTERY"

Keats's revisions, then, bring to the fore problems implicit in the original, above all, how are we to interpret the protagonist's account of his dream? So far as the power of the poem lies in its mystery, revisions contributing to increased ambiguity or ambivalence strengthen its power rather than weakening it. That mystery is central to the poem is implied even by the changes Keats made within the original letter, as when he excised "death's" from lines one and three of stanza three, thus making the protagonist's fate less sure, or when in stanza four he transformed "Wilds" into "Meads," thereby placing the lady in a less threatening environment. In the letter version we may even be unsure as to who speaks the third and fourth lines of the first two stanzas, since the punctuation would allow them to be responses by the protagonist to the questioner, so that we must be uncertain as to whether the final lines repeat the protagonist's or inquirer's words.

The crucial point, however, for all critiques of "La Belle

Dame" is whether the protagonist's dream gives insight into the truth that the lady is a destructive enchantress, or whether it is an account whose truth is the revelation of his self-deceptive and perhaps self-destructive fear and/or guilt. Thus, for another example, one can think of more than a single reason for his dreaming of "starv'd lips" because we have been told the lady had offered him "relish Sweet / Honey wild and manna dew." All in all, the revisions in the poem tend to intensify our awareness that the speaker may have been malevolently enchanted *or* that he may be wretched because he has denied himself the enjoyment of a truly magical experience. Once the force of such irresolvable doubt has come home to us, the poem becomes more interesting, for its ambiguities gain significance. The sadness of the lady, for example, might arise from her foreknowledge of the transiency of the passion she feeds. An anonymous reviewer more than a century ago articulated perfectly what the ballad's indeterminacy gains us, when he remarked that Keatsian doubt was not "the denial of any thing, so much as the preserving of all things; the doubt of one who would rather walk in mystery than in false light . . . who prefers the broken fragment of truth to the imposing completeness of a delusion."[11] We can be absolutely sure about nothing in "La Belle Dame," even at points about who is speaking, because the poet can conceive of certainties, such as "there is no magic," as systematic delusions or "false lights" fostered by our society, which may or may not provide us with the best or most complete definitions of reality. The poem, therefore, persistently releases the possibility of inversions of its apparently plain assertions: sure in language strange it tells us true—and one couldn't hope for a more eloquent definition of Romantic Fantasy.

"La Belle Dame Sans Merci," moreover, enables us to understand that, given the disenchanted nature of post-Enlightenment civilization, its dialogic mode of self-questioning is the only effective way to approach the now incredible truths of fantasy. That is to say, the skeptical rationality of post-Enlightenment thinking must be used self-reflexively by the Romantic fantasist. All the appeals to a reader's negative capability in "La Belle Dame" fulfill the function of directing an intelligence hostile to supernaturalism back upon itself. Only thus can an enlightened reader be given access to experience of what his culture defines as incredible, that is, as inexperiencable. Unlike science fiction, which extrapolates from what is assumed to be certain, and does so in a fashion that has come to be regarded as appropriate for conveying certainty—namely, reportorial lucidity—Romantic fantasy both substantively and formally must be self-doubting and self-threatening, because it seeks discovery of a magicality that has been scientifically proved cannot exist.

CHAPTER FOUR

Exploiting Balladry

It seems to me that we know, despite the say-nothing wisdom
of the metaphysicians, too little, or nearly nothing at all about
the true nature of space to consider as *absolutely impossible*
that which appears to us unnatural.

CARL FRIEDRICH GAUSS

 OTH "THE ANCIENT MARINER" AND "LA BELLE DAME"
were partly inspired by resistance to Word-
sworthian naturalistic lyrical balladry. Yet
however much Coleridge's and Keats's ballads differ from "The Idiot Boy" and "Peter
Bell," all four are alike in not imitating but
exploiting balladic art.[1] Coleridge's and
Keats's anti-Wordsworthian impulses, therefore, need to be situated within a larger context of Romantic and post-Romantic
creative transformations of the popular ballad form. Coleridge's
and Keats's balladic supernaturalism is far profounder and more
complicated than the supernaturalism of genuine ballads. But,
despite the praise that has been lavished on "La Belle Dame" and
"The Ancient Mariner," their supernaturalism was to be no more
favored by post-Romantic poets than by Wordsworth. The
predominate use made of the balladic form since the beginning
of the nineteenth century has followed Wordsworth's lead, away
from the fantasy ballad.

HOUSMAN AND KEATS

Illustrative of post-Romantic tendencies is the practice of A. E.
Housman, whom Friedman cites as the post-Romantic poet who
most significantly used balladic forms.[2]

"Is my team ploughing,
    That I was used to drive
And hear the harness jingle
    When I was man alive?"

Ay, the horses trample,
    The harness jingles now;
No change though you lie under
    The land you used to plough.

"Is football playing
    Along the river shore,
With lads to chase the leather,
    Now I stand up no more?"

Ay, the ball is flying,
    The lads play heart and soul;
The goal stands up, the keeper
    Stands up to keep the goal.

"Is my girl happy,
    That I thought hard to leave,
And has she tired of weeping
    As she lies down at eve?"

Ay, she lies down lightly,
    She lies not down to weep:
Your girl is well contented.
    Be still, my lad, and sleep.

"Is my friend hearty,
    Now I am thin and pine,
And has he found to sleep in
    A better bed than mine?"

Yes, lad, I lie easy,
    I lie as lads would choose;
I cheer a dead man's sweetheart,
    Never ask me whose.

"Is my team ploughing" is characteristic of a good many nineteenth- and twentieth-century lyrics that utilize a balladic form for simplicity and directness of manner as well as a popular tone. Ballad measure may provide Housman a justification for the device of the dead man speaking, but he doesn't emphasize the supernaturalism of that circumstance, any more than he focuses our attention on the ballad form as form. "The Ancient Mariner" and "La Belle Dame" call our attention to their balladic qualities both stylistic and substantive, but readers of Housman's seem seldom to have considered important that it conforms to balladic conventions of dialogue. Readers may easily forget that the poem is a ballad because it is not self-questioning—the form is merely a vehicle. Housman uses ballad measure as appropriate to rendering a vision of the natural course of things. Even the final surprise of the dead man being the former lover only manifests another natural continuity.

Housman's lyric, in theme and form, alerts us to how unusual is "La Belle Dame's" stress on the unnatural, on what is inherently mysterious. The stanzas of "Is my team ploughing" are consistently regular, whereas Keats shortens the fourth line of his quatrains: by thus jarring us with the abbreviation of a simple, brief stanza he reminds us of the form of his poem. Whereas Housman's diction is deliberately commonplace, Keats uses odd, exotic, archaic words, even employing the old French title for his lady. "Is my team ploughing" is a unified utterance, all of a piece, even to its linear progress. Keats's circling poem might well be called a diachronic dialogue, for it is constituted of diction characteristic of and references to diverse times and conditions (and hence different languages) of life; it is even possible that the two speakers in the poem belong to quite different eras, for one can be no more certain of how long the protagonist has been "sojurning" than of how long the Ancient Mariner has been wandering.

There is no need for Housman to make changes like Keats's revision of "has withered" to "is withered" so as further to destabilize simple chronology, nor is there place in Housman's poem for the self-quizzing dubiety of "as she did love," the oxymoron of "sweet moan," in short, for "language strange."

Strange language is appropriate in Keats's poem because it deals with an unreal reality, something other than the natural course of things. Keats encourages our attention to the artifices of his presentation, keeping us aware of reading an archaistic reconstruction of a popular form. Questionableness of his poem's form as well as its content is made integral to our response, posing for us the query that underlies all Romantic fantasy, why fantasize?

GOODY BLAKE MEETS LA BELLE DAME

The contrast with Housman may help us to appreciate Keats's resistance to Wordsworth's naturalistic balladry. The poet in "Peter Bell," for example, represents himself as a teller to unsophisticated country folk of a tale that seems to claim equivalency with a common ballad, although in fact "Peter Bell" possesses all the art Wordsworth could get into it through long and careful revising. He wanted to prove, as he said in his dedication to Southey on the poem's publication in 1819, "that the Imagination not only does not require for its exercise the intervention of supernatural agency, but that, though such agency be excluded, the faculty may be called for as imperiously . . . and for kindred results of Pleasure, by incidents within the compass of poetic probability, in the humblest department of daily life."[3] Whether or not "The Ancient Mariner" was, as I've suggested, inspired by resistance to Wordsworth, these words make it plain that "Peter Bell" might be called anti-Coleridgean. One might even argue that these words confess to the primacy of the supernatural in calling forth imagination, for Wordsworth claims no more for the incidents within "the compass" of "probability" and "daily life" he celebrates than that they compel imagination "*as* imperiously" and reward with "*kindred*" pleasures. At the least, supernatural agency for Wordsworth is a potentiality to be reckoned with: the division between him and Coleridge, reanimated I believe by Keats, represents a significant point of self-conflict within Romanticism.

This natural-supernatural competition reminds us of Wordsworth's one contribution to the original *Lyrical Ballads* that

might seem classifiable as fantastic, that seems to encroach on
Coleridge's domain, "Goody Blake and Harry Gill." But Wordsworth asserted vehemently that this tale was not fantasy. He
cited Erasmus Darwin as his "scientific" source of the literal truth
of the tale of the poor old woman caught stealing sticks from a
prosperous farmer's hedge, and whose prayer that the farmer
may never again feel warm is miraculously granted.[4] The poem
illustrates beautifully the chasm between traditional beliefs and
enlightened skepticism out of which the faint "unfather'd va-
pour" of Romantic fantasy arose. Wordsworth, rather like
Charles Dickens insisting on the factuality of Krook's
spontaneous combustion in *Bleak House*, claims that "Goody
Blake and Harry Gill" reports literal truth, and so his purpose
cannot be to urge belief in the miraculous or providential
character of the preternatural event he records. There is, in
consequence, some logical force to the enlightened conventionality of Southey's objection to the poem.

> The story of a man who suffers the perpetual pain of
> cold because an old woman prayed that he might never
> be warm, is perhaps a good story for a ballad, . . . but is
> the author certain that it is "well authenticated?" And
> does not such an assertion promote the popular
> superstition of witchcraft?[5]

That even Southey wouldn't think of bringing such a charge
against "La Belle Dame" testifies that a fundamental difference
between Wordsworth's ballad and Keats's lies in the former
presenting itself as something like a genuine ballad in appealing
to simple credulity, while the later poem emphasizes its artful
redeploying of balladic characteristics, overtly appealing to a
skeptical intelligence in a reader who would dismiss as mere
fantasy such a tale in more authentically popular form, one
appealing directly to naive belief.

In fact, most of us now are surprised by Southey's critique of
"Goody Blake," because we automatically interpret Wordsworth's poem psychologically, that being for us the only way we
can take the verses seriously. The possibility of a miraculous act
does not even enter our minds, especially since Wordsworth

seems so acutely to have diagnosed the potency (and the means of induction) of a psychosomatic illness. Our psychologizing, of course, involves us in reading the poem naturalistically; we identify the cause of Harry's chill in terms of entirely natural, albeit psychological, processes. "La Belle Dame" does not encourage any such naturalistic interpretation that will explain away its fantastic features, yet simultaneously it makes no elaborate claim (as Wordsworth does for his poem) to simple credulity. This difference is highlighted by the different attitudes of the poets toward their ballads; Keats, as we have noted, making jokes about his, whereas Wordsworth solemnly proclaimed that "Goody Blake" had valuable practical effects on rural readers.

Indeed, a certain Reverend Burney when "Goody Blake" first appeared objected to it (as he could not have objected to "La Belle Dame") not on religious grounds like Southey but on political ones.

> Distress from poverty and want is admirably described in the true story of "Goody Blake and Harry Gill": but are we to imagine that Harry was bewitched by Goody Blake? the hardest heart must be softened into pity for the poor old woman; and yet, if all the poor are to help themselves, and supply their wants from the possessions of their neighbours, what imaginary wants and real anarchy would it not create? Goody Blake should have been relieved of the two millions annually allowed by the state to the poor of this country, not by the plunder of an individual.[6]

Wordsworth lent a degree of legitimacy to Burney's lucid if naive argument by his assertion in the Preface to *Lyrical Ballads* of 1800 that he wished in the poem to draw attention to the power of the imagination to work changes in our "physical nature as might almost appear miraculous." He adds:

> The truth is an important one; the fact (for it is a *fact*) is a valuable illustration of it. And I have the satisfaction of knowing that it has been communicated to many hundreds of people who would never have heard of it,

had it not been narrated as a Ballad, and in a more
impressive metre than is usual in Ballads.[7]

This defines exactly Romantic interest in exploiting balladry,
making the form more impressive. But Wordsworth's aim, and
according to him his success, lies in utilizing the popularity of the
genre to establish a natural truth. Keats and Coleridge exploited
the ballad to establish another kind of truth. Wordsworth, one
must suspect, exaggerated the influence of his poem, but no one
would claim Keats's ballad aims at or is capable of any such
practical effects. The familiar charge that fantasy is escapist,
then, is to a degree valid against the Keatsian kind of ballad so far
as fantasy is, indeed, deliberately a-ideological. Its intrinsic
nature excludes it from the kind of effectiveness Wordsworth was
pleased to think his ballad attained. Oxymoron is not the ideal
mode for political statements. This is why for Keats, who wrestled
with the question of what the social function of poetry ought to
be, fantasy could never have been an easy choice. The fantasist
too obviously is no sage or physician; it seems doubtful that he is
entitled to any moral standing at all.

BLAKE'S ANTIFANTASY

The importance of the a-ideological status of fantasy is perhaps
best dramatized by the work of William Blake, whose imaginative-
ness and skill as a lyricist few today would deny. But Blake never
wrote fantasy. The miraculous events this devoutly Protestant
poet represents, many of them revelatory of his passionate
political commitments, are incredible only to those who have
discarded religious belief. This is why little Tom Dacre's vision of
liberated child laborers in "The Chimney Sweeper" can only be a
dream, a representation of what is not actual reality, for Tom
lives in a modern society in which "all" do not do their duty,
including the reader, for Tom and his pious chum sweep "your"
chimneys. In the London of the 1790s, as Blake's "London"
makes scarifyingly clear, Tom's religious dream is not going to be
realized. The force of "The Chimney Sweeper" arises in good
measure from the clarity with which it defines the antagonistic

separateness of present actualities and the social-political transformation Blake desired.

"Goody Blake" seems less effective as a social critique than
Blake's poem, dramatizing so painfully what conditions ought to
prevail but don't, because Wordsworth's ballad *is*, despite his
disclaimer, a fantastic one. Goody's words do have magical
power; she does cast a real spell. Blake's sweep can only dream.
Blake is ideologically effective because he does not fantasize. His
poem outrages us, inflames us against the real injustice with
which the little sweeps are compelled to learn to live. Blake writes
from the basis of—and in order to articulate—a comprehensive
system of practical improvement. His disdain for the fantastic is a
symptom of an inflexibility in his art that gives it a strength
exactly contrary to that of Keats's unsystematized, fluid, self-
destabilizing art. The difference is neatly focused by a contrast of
Blake's "The Crystal Cabinet" with "La Belle Dame," for there
are potent parallels between the lyrics.

> The Maiden caught me in the Wild
> Where I was dancing merrily
> She put me into her Cabinet
> And Locked me up with a golden key
>
> This Cabinet is formd of Gold
> And Pearl & Crystal shining bright
> And within it opens into a World
> And a little lovely Moony Night
>
> Another England there I saw
> Another London with its Tower
> Another Thames & other Hills
> And another pleasant Surrey Bower
>
> Another Maiden like herself
> Translucent lovely shining clear
> Threefold each in the other closed
> O what a pleasant trembling fear

O what a smile a threefold Smile
Filld me that like a flame I burnd
I bent to Kiss the lovely Maid
And found a Threefold Kiss returnd

I strove to sieze the inmost Form
With ardor fierce & hands of flame
But burst the Crystal Cabinet
And like a Weeping Babe became

A weeping Babe upon the wild
And Weeping Woman pale reclind
And in the outward air again
I filled with woes the passing Wind[8]

The interpretive difficulties in Blake's lyric spring, paradoxically, from its crystalline transparence. If as interpreters we are provoked by "The Crystal Cabinet," it is by the fashion in which its glittering simplicity turns us back into the system of which it seems so lucid an expression. Commentators like Harold Bloom, for instance, immediately explain the term "threefold" in lines 15, 17, and 20 as referring to Blake's conception of "Beulah." The commentator, that is, reads the poem through an understanding of an underlying Blakean system, intellectual, religious, cosmological. No one would think of interpreting "La Belle Dame" by reference to some such elaborate Keatsian system. Blake's poem, moreover, presents itself as a comprehensible sequential structure, appearing as if a coherent organization of causes and effects. This seeming intrinsic firmness contributes to the poem's strongly moralistic tone, as when the maiden vanishes because the speaker tries to seize her. Like the cabinet, the lyric, focusing on a human artifact, appears to be an elegantly self-enclosed construct, perfect in its essential form.

The variety of interpretations it has provoked, however, proves that this transparency is a kind of trick, energized by the poem's words' consistently misleading suggestion that they refer to plainly definable causal processes. And the verb tenses support our sense of meeting with clear-cut effects, for the experience represented is unmistakably *past*. The dancing speaker has become like a "weeping Babe" as he fills "with woes the passing Wind." The lyric treats of some process, however circular, that has finished one cycle and so is capable of definitive ordering. The lines' strong repetitions further tempt us to believe that we can easily find a rational explanation for the total event. In fact, of course, the poem is not so easy to interpret, but that it appears so distinguishes it from "La Belle Dame," which presents itself as uncertain, indeterminate, opaque.

Keats's poem begins and ends in the present, so that in a sense it remains unfinished, incomplete, particularly since the speaker's story does not seem, like that of Blake's dancer, logically self-sufficient. What Blake's poem tells of is as impossible as what Keats's poem tells of, but Blake's *telling* appears straightforward, virtually didactic. The event's unlikelihood is not foregrounded, so we are tempted to treat what is impossible in the poem as symbolic or allegorical, as representing something more possible. We accept Blake's poem's strangeness as a sign of a complex underlying logical structure. The key action in Keats's poem, to the contrary, is uncertain and arouses in us uncertainty—if dream, what kind of dream?—so that direct allegorizing or symbolizing is not an attractive interpretive option. We wonder if the protagonist is victim or victimizer. We are caught up into a confusing process rather than confronted by definitive results. Unsure of who is speaking at some points, bewildered by a seeming interpenetration of different kinds of existence, we feel Keats's protagonist may be mistaken about his facts (something that does not so readily occur to us with Blake's dancer) and that we will never be absolutely sure what ails him, even if we analyze carefully the poem's concealed structure. On the opposite side, we feel that we can understand what the woes of Blake's speaker are, and we puzzle only how to interpret them, what they may "stand for," may represent. To state the contrast starkly in terms of theme: Blake's dancer has clearly failed in his aspiration, but we wonder if Keats's protagonist has failed. Has he escaped? Or is his ailment that he has succeeded in escaping?

Blake's poem, although implying an environment of repetitiveness and cyclic sorrow, in itself moves linearly, advancing

logically from speaker as dancer to speaker as lamenter, with the
hunted predatory Maiden complementarily transforming into
Weeping Woman. Keats's poem, though treating a singular
event, moves in an irregularly circular fashion, incompletely
reflecting the recursive dialogue in which, for example, the final
words create a problem of interpretation, "this is why" simply
carrying us back into the story whose meaning has already baffled
us. These contrasts are refracted in spatial and locational differences, for the natural world in Blake's lyric is simply "the Wild,"
and everything that exists outside the crystal cabinet seems
imaged or able to be imaged within it. Our attention is thus
concentrated on the cabinet, the miniaturizing artifact. All of
"La Belle Dame" takes place out of doors, although "nature" here
contains the threat at least of ahuman forces. If the lady is
demonic, her demonism is of and in a "natural" realm whose
limits are treacherously vague. A faery's child may be dangerous
to a human, as in a different fashion a wild animal may be, but
the threat makes neither animal nor fairy unnatural. In short,
Blake's poem exists within a totally humanized world, or one that
could be totally humanized, whereas Keats thrusts us into an
environment that includes what is genuinely strange.

Blake's maiden seems no fairy creature, but a symbolic
representation of something potential in any normal woman;
"The Crystal Cabinet" does not strike us as fantastic, because its
characters are not presented as alien beings. Blake's poem,
therefore, is much more complex than it may at first appear to
be, but its complexity, what makes it interesting, is precisely that
there is nothing *mysterious* in it, nothing outside the system of
the poem as—plainly enough—a human artifact. One might
guess even from this little lyric that what others see as dark and
menacing aspects of an outside world, Blake sees as no more than
projections of human fears and blindnesses. For Keats, however,
the natural world contains true mystery, what is nonhuman,
beyond definition by our systems, and not exorcisable by
psychological analysis.

These various differences suggest how profoundly significant
is the a-ideological character of Romantic fantasy. From a
Blakean perspective, Keats *should* be regarded as an escapist,

even if one treats the conventional pejorative connotations of escapism with caution. Romantic fantasy is composed in the wake of societal developments entailing destruction of magicality, so fantasy must escape this destruction by trying to recover through sheer literary accomplishment the equivalent of attitudes and beliefs fallen out of favor, degraded, or forgotten. The Romantic fantasist does strive indeed to create something, therefore, quite different from the accepted reality within which he lives and his creative impulse originated. He is guided by a desire for what does not exist unless he brings it into being. So, finally, "escapism" is exactly the wrong term for Romantic fantasy, which requires the invention of what the artist cannot find in the circumstances of now normal life, that his fellows even deny should or could exist.

THE SHAKESPEARIAN AUTHORIZATION

Tobin Siebers has demonstrated persuasively how the Enlightenment's demolition of superstition led to Romantic fantasies based on writers' adopting the viewpoint of victims of the new dispensation.[9] Fantasy deliberately upsets systems of enlightened progressivity, and is charged, not surprisingly, with being regressive. Nor unjustly. The creation by Keats of a ballad such as "La Belle Dame" in post-Napoleonic England resurrects a kind of creature banished by modern civilization, though so to imagine her may be a sign of an effort to expand sympathies narrowed and diminished by rationalized progress.

Siebers works principally with Continental fantasy, so he ignores the powerful sense an Englishman like Keats felt that he was repossessing an important native literary tradition. In the British tradition there was a place, an honored place, for the fantastic, distinguishing its "northern" art from classical, Mediterranean, latinate traditions. For the English Romantics the greatest of writers, of course, was Shakespeare, an Englishman, a popular poet, and one whose work included many elements of fantasy.

Plays such as A *Midsummer's Night Dream* and *The Tempest*, however popular, were regarded as in no sense primitive or unsophisticated by the Romantics. These dramas, as much as *Hamlet* or *Lear*, were cited in support of the Coleridgean argument that Shakespeare's judgment and technical skills were equal to his immense power of vision and capacity to arouse emotion. This British appreciation of Shakespeare sustains the Romantics' willingness to attempt fantasy, particularly because the Romantics also admired Shakespeare's sensitivity to the life of ordinary people, his intuitive sympathy with the nature of the beliefs, fears, aspirations, and superstitions of common folk.

Shakespeare's plays above all else explain why the great ballads of Coleridge and Keats, two intensely literary poets, differ so strikingly from the ballads of most Romantic poets in other national traditions (especialy, of course, those of the Germans). Even the English poets feeling no compulsion to practice extensively in this genre owes something to the presence of Shakespeare. His example for the Romantics proved beyond cavil or need for defensive assertion that the native British tradition included the possibility of high aesthetic accomplishment through exploitation of popular literary forms and unsophisticated, superstitious attitudes of mind. Again, the key term is *exploitation*. "The Ancient Mariner" and "La Belle Dame" are no mere imitations of popular balladry, anymore than *A Midsummer's Night Dream* imitates folk beliefs. The Romantic ballads bring to life a vision hinted at but mostly unrealized in actual popular ballads. Such retrieval, the Romantics thought, had been exemplified in Shakespeare's superb dramatic utilizations of popular forms and ways of thought. What the English Romantics made of balladic modes implies their desire not to improve them but to see through them so as to make effective what the ballads treat feebly, clumsily, uncomprehendingly. The English Romantics' dissatisfaction with ordinary ballads arises less from regarding them as unsophisticated and lacking in polish, than from perceiving them as not fully dramatizing the potential fully revealed only by Shakespeare's magnificent artistry. "The Ancient Mariner" and "La Belle Dame," in fact, radically rework the popular ballads' most characteristic qualities so as to overcome their inadequate expressions of the power their form could manifest, just as, one might say, *The Tempest* attains

truly magical power seldom if ever manifested in popular superstitions.[10]

DEMON LOVER AND TRUE THOMAS

The essence of Romantic ballad-reworking under the aegis of
Shakespeare's genius appears in its application to materials of
popular balladry an intensely critical intelligence. Only by such
self-conscious criticism could potentialities hidden within the
artistic insufficiency of ordinary ballads be realized. The process
may be illustrated by contrasting Keats's ballad with a representative popular ballad, such as "The Demon Lover," which has been
cited as a possible source for "La Belle Dame."

> "O where have you been my long, long love,
>   This long seven years and more?"
> "Oh I'm come to seek my former vows,
>   Ye granted me before."
>
> "O hold your tongue of your former vows,
>   For they will breed sad strife;
> O hold your tongue of your former vows,
>   For I am become a wife."
>
> He turned him right and round about,
>   And the tear blinded his ee;
> "I wad never hae trodden on Irish ground,
>   If it had not been for thee.
>
> "I might have had a king's daughter,
>   Far far beyond the sea;
> I might have had a king's daughter,
>   Had it not been for love o' thee."
>
> "If ye might have had a king's daughter,
>   Yersell ye had to blame;
> Ye might have taken the king's daughter,
>   For ye kend that I was nane."

"O faulse are the vows o' womankind,
    But fair is their faulse bodie;
I never wad hae trodden on Irish ground,
    Had it not been for love o' thee."

"If I was to leave my husband dear,
    And my two babes also,
O what have you to take me to,
    If with you I should go?"

"I have seven ships upon the sea,
    The eighth brought me to land;
With four-and-twenty bold mariners,
    And music on every hand."

She has taken up her two little babes,
    Kiss'd them baith cheek and chin;
"O fare ye weel, my ain two babes,
    For I'll never see you again."

She set her foot upon the ship,
    No mariners could she behold;
But the sails were o' the taffetie,
    And the mast o' the beaten gold.,

She had not sailed a league, a league
    A league, but barely three,
When dismal grew his countenance,
    And drumlie grew his ee.

The masts that were like the beaten gold,
    Bent not on the heaving seas;
But the sails, that were o' the taffetie,
    Filled not in the east land breeze.

They had not sail'd a league, a league,
    A league, but barely three,
Until she espied his cloven foot,
    And she wept right bitterlie.

"O hold you tongue of your weeping," says he,
    "Of your weeping now let me be;
"I will show how the lilies grow
        On the banks of Italy."

"O what hills are yon, yon pleasant hills,
    That the sun shines sweetly on?"
"O yon are the hills of heaven," he said,
    "Where you will never win."

"O whaten a mountain is yon," she said,
    "All so dreary wi' frost and snow?"
"O yon is the mountain of hell," he cried,
    Where you and I will go."

And aye when she turn'd her round about,
    Aye taller he seemed for to be;
Until that the tops o' the gallant ship
    Nae taller were than he.

The clouds grew dark and the wind grew loud,
    And the levin fill'd her ee;
And waesome wail'd the snaw-white sprites,
    Upon the gurlie sea.

He struck the tapmast wi' his hand,
    The foremast wi' his knee;
And he brak that gallant ship in twain,
    And sank her in the sea.[11]

    This ballad divides into two distinct parts. The first nine
stanzas present a realistic dialogue of a woman yielding to the
appeal of a former lover, while the last ten portray her supernatural punishment by the devil. Since there can hardly be a question
of the justice of her fate, the potential psychosocial complexity of
the first half of the ballad seems betrayed by the moral rigorous-
ness of the second half. Even in ballads that do not so neatly
separate their elements, one frequently encounters an analogous

constriction of psychological, social, even political complexity within conventionalized moral limits. This rigorous containment of implications is one source of balladic charm, to be sure, but it cuts off that profundity of questioning, especially self-questioning, a potential development of strangeness, that Romantic poets desired. Aesthetic-moral stylizing, apparent in many fairy tales and other genre of folk literature, has tempted modern structuralists into elaborate analyses of such popular forms. These analyses, whatever their value to linguists and folklorists, are impotent to describe the effects attained by "La Belle Dame." They are impotent because Keats's poem *escapes* balladic conventionality by exploring through opportunities contained within the form itself the possible significance of that "strangeness" of which the first nine stanzas of "The Demon Lover" are representative. If one wonders about the woman's judgment when she gives up a respectable and responsible marriage to return to a lover she knows to be faithless, one is baffled by the moral status of Keats's Belle Dame. The moral closure enforced by "The Demon Lover" in its final stanzas has been reopened by Keats. His poem does not embody confirmatory judgment but is a means for searching after ethical conviction. "La Belle Dame" discards the moralistic half of the genuine ballad to press deeper into darkly disturbing possibilities of self-destruction—subterraneously present but not fully articulated—in the first portion of "The Demon Lover." It is Keats's skepticism, his intelligent resistance to easy acceptance of conventional forms and beliefs, that allows him to release through his deliberate—and overtly displayed—archaizing artistry complexities the traditional ballad conceals. By intensifying the undeveloped problematic lurking within the form the poet seems to revive, the Romantic fantasist in fact transforms his model into a newly self-reflexive form capable, as no genuine ballad could be, of challenging the disenchanted condition in which he composes.

A more likely direct source for Keats's poem is the justly famous "True Thomas" or "Thomas the Rhymer," which ballad specialists identify as belonging to an earlier stratum of balladic history than "The Demon Lover." Be that as it may, "Thomas

the Rhymer" is a complicated poem, full of surprising ambiguities, though it does seem unequivocally to identify Elfland as
attainable by a road leading neither to heaven nor hell.

> True Thomas lay on Huntlie bank;
>   A ferlie he spied wi' his ee;
> And there he saw a ladye bright,
>   Come riding down by the Eildon Tree.
>
> Her shirt was o' the grass-green silk,
>   Her mantle o' the velvet fyne;
> At ilka tett of her horse's mane,
>   Hang fifty siller bells and nine.
>
> True Thomas, he pull'd aff his cap,
>   And louted low down to his knee,
> "All hail, thou mighty Queen of Heaven!
>   For thy peer on earth I never did see."
>
> "O no, O no, Thomas," she said;
>   "That name does not belang to me;
> I am but the Queen of fair Elfland,
>   That am hither come to visit thee."
>
> "Harp and carp, Thomas," she said
>   "Harp and carp along wi' me;
> And if ye dare to kiss my lips
>   Sure of your bodie I will be."
>
> Betide me weal, betide me woe,
>   That weird shall never daunton me."
> Syne he has kissed her rosy lips,
>   All underneath the eildon tree.
>
> "Now, ye maun go wi' me,' she said;
>   'True Thomas, ye maun go wi' me;
> And ye maun serve me seven years,
>   Thro' weal or woe as may chance to be."

She mounted on her milk-white steed;
    She's ta'en true Thomas up behind;
And aye, whene'er her bridle rung,
    The steed flew swifter than the wind.

O they rade on, and farther one
    The steed gaed swifter than the wind;
Until they reached a desert wide,
    And living land was left behind.

"Light down, light down, now, true Thomas,
    And lean your head upon my knee:
Abide and rest a little space,
    And I will show you ferlies three.

"O see ye not yon narrow road,
    So thick beset with thorns and briers?
That is the path of righteousness,
    Though after it but few inquires.

"And see ye not that braid braid road,
    That lies across that lily leven?
That is the path of wickedness,
    Though some call it the road to Heaven.

"And see ye not that bonny road
    That winds about the fernie brae?
That is the road to fair Elfland
    Where thou and I this night maun gae.

"But, Thomas, ye maun hold your tongue,
    Whatever ye may hear or see;
For, if you speak word in Elfyn land,
    Ye'll ne'er get back to your ain countrie."

O they rade on, and farther on,
    And they waded through rivers aboon the knee,
And they saw neither sun nor moon,
    But they heard the roaring of the sea.

It was a mirk mirk night, and there was nae stern light,
　　And they waded through red blude to the knee;
For a' the blude, that's shed on earth,
　　Rins through the springs o' that countrie.

Syne they came on to a garden green
　　And she pu'd an apple frae a tree—
"Take this for thy wages, true Thomas;
　　It will give thee the tongue that can never lie."

"My tongue is mine ain," true Thomas said;
　　"A gudely gift ye wad gie to me!
I neither dought to buy nor sell,
　　At fair or tryst where I may be.

"I dought neither speak to prince or peer,
　　Nor ask of grace from fair ladye."
"Now hold thy peace!" the ladye said,
　　"For as I say, so must it be."

He has gotten a coat of the even cloth,
　　And a pair of shoes of velvet green;
And, till seven years were gane and past,
　　True Thomas on earth was never seen.[12]

It is this ballad that Tolkien cites as evidence that Elfland is part
of our world, not a different realm, however unlike it may be to
those portions of the globe with which we are familiar.[13] But it is
the injunctions put on Thomas, along with his responses, that
many readers have found most puzzling. Offered an apple that
"will give thee the tongue that can never lie,"—true apple or false
like that dishonestly urged in another garden?—he replies,
having previously been warned that he must not speak in Elfland,
"my tongue is mine ain," and that "I neither dought to buy nor
sell . . . nor ask of grace from fair ladye." Does *true* Thomas say
that one needs a lying tongue to buy, sell, woo—to be a humanly
social being? Doubtfulness as to his meaning is congruent with
the ambivalent quality of the Queen of Elfland, whose tyranny
rewards plain-speaking Thomas not only with clothing of a

wealthy and powerful person, but, according to tradition, prophetic powers upon his return to earth.

   This ballad intrigues us by its surprising turning back upon
itself, by leading us to rethink the ideas we have brought to it
about plain speaking and the articulation of truth. "Thomas the
Rhymer" is somewhat unusual among genuine popular ballads
both in its involuted complexity and its overt centering on
problems of speaking and being silent, on how truth may be less
simple than it first appears, and how the integrity of a speaker—
"my tongue is mine ain" (but, the ballad forces us to ask, is
it?)—may be judged differently depending on where, when, and
within what circumstances one speaks out or holds one's tongue.
By thus bringing into question the very linguistic foundation of
strict moralizing of the conventional ballad, "Thomas the
Rhymer" may even be said to be about balladry. It is this
reflexivity that Keats develops brilliantly in "La Belle Dame."
Keats redoubles the ambivalences in "Thomas the Rhymer" by
increasing our uncertainty as to the validity of the protagonist's
report of his adventure with a lady whose magical powers are
perhaps even more dubious than those of the Queen of Elfland. I
share the view of those who think Keats's ballad owes something
to "Thomas the Rhymer," yet any such indebtedness calls
attention to how far Keats's poem advances beyond it. "La Belle
Dame" surpasses "Thomas the Rhymer" by critically testing the
power of balladic form through Keats's adroit deployment of its
structural conventions, rhetorical techniques, and dictional
characteristics so as to evoke the wonder of what his society
regards as unnatural and therefore incredible.

   The superior involuting intensity of Keats's poem is necessi-
tated by his effort to discover, within the disenchanted realm of
skeptical modernism in which he lives and composes his poetry,
means of dramatizing what is other than the human, to what
Tolkien was to give the generic name of "Elfland." This is a task
no popular ballad undertakes, for such a ballad is created under
"conditions of credulity," wherein superstition is, or can be
treated as being, a vitally shared reality. Seeking the authentically
strange within cultural circumstances that recognize nothing
nonhuman as of real importance, Keats does not search for

something fundamental or essential deep within our humanness. What is fantastic in "La Belle Dame" and "The Ancient Mariner" are alternatives to the rational and natural as defined by all-triumphant Enlightened Western European humanity. Because these are poems about encounters with what is different from us, they treat what may be only partially amenable to articulation in language. The art of "La Belle Dame" (like that of "The Ancient Mariner") in consequence must evoke what in the ordinary terms of modern converse as well as those of highly sophisticated psychological analysis will not make good sense. Romantic fantasy does not even have the justification of making strange everyday phenomena; Romantic fantasy does not defamiliarize the commonplace so that we may perceive the usual with its veil of familiarity torn off. It attempts, rather, the highly peculiar task of creating awareness that what we have come to accept as the only possible reality may not be as absolute, complete, or comprehensive as we think, and of urging us to imagine what in a progressive and enlightened and incredulous world must seem inconceivable.

CHAPTER FIVE

Mariner's Rime to Freud's Uncanny

Unlike other national literatures in which the fantastic appears
only as a marginal manifestation, English literature . . . is in
reality the chosen land of fantastic literature.

JULIO CORTAZAR,
"The Recent State of Fiction in Latin America"

UALITIES THAT MAKE "THE RIME OF THE ANCIENT
Mariner" successful fantasy may be high-
lighted by contrasting the ballad with Robert
Browning's celebrated monologue written
half a century later, "Childe Roland to the
Dark Tower Came." Browning's poem illustrates how Romantic fantasy was psycho-
logized and transformed into a more symbolic art. Another half
century later this process of domesticating the strange culmi-
nated in Freud's essay "The Uncanny."

The reader of "Childe Roland" is confronted with puzzles,
questions, and riddles that are overtly puzzles, questions, and
riddles. The reader is at once and throughout his reading forced
to interpret, to ask: what does this detail really mean? We read the
poem as an enigma. Although finally "The Ancient Mariner"
may pose profounder difficulties for a critical analyst, almost
nothing in the poem is presented to the reader as enigmatic.
Coleridge's poem seems to demand only that we listen to its
"rime." Consider "Life-in-Death":

> Her lips were red, her looks were free,
> Her locks were yellow as gold:
> Her skin was white as leprosy
> The Night-mare Life-in-Death was she,
> Who thicks man's blood with cold.[1]

The weird figure who thus so unexpectedly appears as if every reader were sure to recognize her—and she is so accepted by the gloss—is in fact quite mysterious. At least to my knowledge no one has explained exactly who she is or precisely where she comes from. Even John Livingston Lowes' research is of little help with her. Yet the lack of critical remark on the strangeness of Life-in-Death indicates how unemphasized is her enigmatic quality. Some of the magicality of "The Ancient Mariner" derives from its presentation of the mysterious as if commonplace; as in genuine ballads the mysterious is taken for granted. Strangeness and inconsistencies are concealed by the apparent simple surface of Coleridge's ballad. The poem by its seeming transparency disarms our tendency to probe for explanations, that disarming being a principal constituent of the spell it casts.

One feature of this technique for preempting skeptical analysis is the suppression of allusions; the poem represents itself as existing without significant intertextual connections. This trait, too, is thrown into high relief by the contrast of "Childe Roland," whose title is immediately followed by the adjuration, "See Edgar's Song in *King Lear.*" Such literary allusiveness appears nowhere in Coleridge's ballad. Lowes' *Road to Xanadu* demonstrated that "The Ancient Mariner" draws deeply on Coleridge's incomparably extensive reading, although the poem never addresses a reader's familiarity with other writing.[2] Lowes' laborious scholarship was required to reveal the sources of Coleridge's art because "The Ancient Mariner" so successfully, however duplicitously, presents itself as naively unliterary, like a truly anonymous popular ballad. This deceptive appearance was enhanced by Coleridge's late addition of a more "sophisticated" yet quaintly "learned" gloss that treats the balladic narrative as unproblematic and requiring no profound interpretation.

QUEST MONOLOGUE AND DIALOGIC NON-QUEST

The unallusiveness of "The Ancient Mariner" is but one aspect of the poem's concealing its potential puzzles within transparency. Browning's poem in an antithetical fashion skillfully teases and tempts the reader to decipher an ostentatiously hidden

significance, emphasizes its puzzling character, insistently fore-
grounds its riddles, just as it explicitly calls attention to possible
literary affiliations. There is an analogous difference between
Coleridge's anonymous seaman and Browning's protagonist, who
is not only named but also given a title that locates him in the
upper strata of society. In the conventional view, at least, what
happens to a knight is more important than what happens to a
nobody. Browning's title indicates, moreover, that by the end of
the poem his knight will have attained something definite, even if
we must guess what the dark tower is or signifies. Coleridge's
protagonist, in contrast, sets off for an undefined destination,
returns to an equally unidentified home, from which he then
moves on to further chance encounters with various auditors.
Browning's title announces a commitment to the recounting of a
quest. To the Mariner, events unexpectedly happen. The Romantic protagonist is no seeker. Whatever else it may be, "The
Ancient Mariner" is not a quest.

    These contrasts derive from the principal formal distinction
between the works: "The Ancient Mariner" is a dialogic narrative, whereas "Childe Roland" is a dramatic monologue. "My first
thought was he lied," Browning's univocal work begins, and
every problem it raises is raised in terms of how it is enunciated
by the monologist. So it is not surprising that some critics treat
everything in the poem as a projection of the Childe's mind. No
such purely psychological reading of Coleridge's poem is appropriate, for it at once and ostentatiously inscribes one narrative
within another:

> It is an ancient Mariner,
> And he stoppeth one of three.
> "By thy long grey beard and glittering eye,
> Now wherefore stopp'st thou me?" (1–4)

The poem's dialogical quality extends beyond a diversity of
conversations and points of view articulated within the poem,
even beyond the glosser's discussion of the original dialogue
between Mariner and Wedding Guest, into the narrative's consistent unpredictability. By unpredictability I do not refer, of
course, to mere suspense, the reader's ignorance of what will

happen next, a narrative attribute of minor significance, since its full effect exists only in a first encounter, but to the ordering of the tale according to nonlinear, nonlogical, self-interruptive modes. Most simply, the story is of a conversation, the intersecting of two utterances, which means that for either speaker the speech of the other is unpredictable. Nor are the connections between the events whose sequence makes up the Mariner's rime obvious and easily understandable. Perhaps the easiest fashion of illustrating the poem's unpredictability vis-à-vis "Childe Roland" is to observe that "The Ancient Mariner" is full of a variety of differentiated conditions and surprising shifts of mood and tone affecting both protagonist and reader. This difference from Browning's poem is concretized by the difference in landscapes. The Mariner undergoes radical shifts in his physical circumstances, traveling through tumultuous arctic seas to oppressive tropic calm back to his pleasantly temperate home port. Roland's landscape is all of a bad piece, as he follows a course that increasingly seems foreordained if not inevitable. And whether the countryside Roland rides through exists objectively or is only a projection of his mind, his progress is a reenacting. He fulfills a preexistent pattern; to himself and to the reader Roland appears as the latest of a series of questers for the same goal. So whatever meaning one ascribes to Browning's poem, it will necessarily be an archetypal one.

"The Ancient Mariner" recounts absolute discovery—" We were the first that ever burst / Into that silent sea" (105–06). Although the Mariner tells us that he repeats his tale (whereas Roland speaks only once), the Mariner's account is of a unique occurrence, not a reenactment. The force of his narrative's significance, whether that is limited to the moral enunciated by the Mariner, or something more, lies in the tale being not archetypal but ectypal. The significance of the Mariner's story is its singularity.

In representing the Mariner's adventures as unique, in telling a dialogical-ectypal story rather than an monologic-archetypal one, Coleridge translated into his astonishingly self-conscious art a primary attribute of popular balladry. Ballads, however derivative and conventionally patterned, present them-

selves as unique. The stories they tell usually are thoroughly
traditional, but they are told as if singular. It is this naive
duplicity which makes appropriate the appending of a moral,
such as "Now lovers all, take heed." And in this respect the moral
of the Mariner is finely appropriate, for it is Coleridge's artistic
enhancement of balladic deceptiveness that renders the Mariner's moral tag for most readers inadequate as an evaluation of
the experience offered by the poem as a whole.[3] Naive deceit is
thus transformed into a conscious device for giving the reader
access to complexities at best hinted at by genuine ballads. Like
"La Belle Dame," "The Ancient Mariner" renders problematic
the form it so brilliantly embodies: formally, it is too good a ballad
to be a true one. The poem's false transparency and superficiality
are functions of its bringing into question the form that it seems
to make so comprehensible. What could be simpler than a ballad?
Yet "The Ancient Mariner" leads every reader to doubts about its
simplicity. This self-testing is, of course, reinforced by the gloss,
which supplies a critical analysis whose charming self-confidence
emphasizes its inadequacies without clarifying the problems
posed by the Mariner's rime. The gloss does no more than
supplement difficulties uncovered by Coleridge's ballad, whose
artifice, whose falsity, is manifested by its appearing so utterly
balladic.

AROUSING A READER'S SUSPICION

If "The Ancient Mariner" leads us into wondering about the
qualities intrinsic to balladic narrative, why are we so much more
distrustful of Roland as he reenacts his quest than of the Mariner
spinning his singular yarn? We are forced to distrust Roland
because he trusts no one, others or himself, a characteristic that
makes him seem more modern than the Mariner. The knight's
unreliability in a treacherous environment, however, is never a
simple matter. His first thought is that the cripple lied, yet Roland
follows the cripple's directions. Why? It would seem to matter
what he asked directions for. After all, if Roland inquired for the
road to the Dark Tower, the countryside into which he is directed
would augur he was headed the right way—as indeed he is. But if

he asked the way to the heavenly city, as has been suggested on the grounds of the poem's indebtedness to Bunyan's *Pilgrim's Progress*, one could hardly blame him for wondering if he had been put on the best road. Or, if he disbelieves the cripple, why follow his advice? But the suspicion endemic to Browning's poem penetrates deeper than malicious misdirection, for the poem, of course, is a monologue, and this form reflects the solipsistic quality of the entire world of the verses. "Childe Roland" represents circumstances in which one must suspect everybody, including oneself and one's suspicions.

So the reader of "Childe Roland" is meant to respond suspiciously. The point of a dramatic monologue is to encourage us to assess skeptically what we overhear. We are intended to distrust what Roland says, just as he distrusts the cripple, even though following his direction, as we follow Roland's thought. Browning tempts us to ask, as Roland asks himself about the cripple's purposes, what is the real, the hidden, the latent significance of the Childe's words? The poem's meaning therefore consists in what we decipher from clues provided by the ostensible meaning of Roland's speech. These words are "surface" phenomena important as symptoms, important only so far as they enable us to discover something else to which by indirection they point, a significance underneath them, interpretable from them only if we apply to them skepticism as to their literal import.

SUPERFICIALITY OF TELLING

Differences of opinion about Coleridge's ballad seem to radiate away from its surface so far as the chief and abiding difficulty posed by the poem is to give credence to the incredible. What is said by Childe Roland is important for its implications that differ from its ostensible meaning. What the Mariner means he says. His simplicity, of course, does not do away with the need for our critical questioning. The challenge posed to an enlightened reader by the Mariner's words, however, is not to probe their unconscious betrayals but how to accept the possibility of such impossible occurrences, first of all, of course, the Mariner's spellbinding power. In our age, *spellbinding* is mere metaphor. For the Wedding Guest, and through him the reader, it becomes literal condition. We cannot respond in any significant way to the poem without accepting the possibility of a power of enchantment we have learned to dismiss as hyperbolic.

We can perhaps better specify the problems of transparency posed by "The Ancient Mariner" if we recognize that the superficiality of the poem is a sign of its dialogic nature, which means that, unlike Roland, the Mariner not only needs a listener but is also needed by a listener. Nobody needs Roland. But someone such as the Mariner is required if one is to test what has become a common conviction, namely, that there is nothing supernatural in our world, that, since nothing happens except by natural processes, we can rationally understand—and thereby control—everything. To define the test from the opposite perspective, if whatever may appear weird, fantastic, or incomprehensible can be reduced to rational intelligibility, what are we to do with the Mariner? The crux of the situation lies in its reciprocal nature: the Mariner needs someone to be spellbound by him, or his "strange power of speech" will remain unexercised, and our strange confidence in our natural rationality will remain untroubled.

The Mariner is provoked into retelling by encountering someone he feels compelled to teach. The Mariner, significantly, though he stops the Wedding Guest, does not speak first; he answers a question—at length—asked by the guest; "Wherefore stopp'st thou me?" when the halt seems made not by physical force but what we now call eye contact. In any event, the Mariner's utterance is not purely spontaneous; it is a rejoinder; it is not primarily expressive. These small yet crucial circumstances show the rime coming into being through an odd reciprocity, which, since Bakhtin, we are inclined to call *dialogic*. This means, in part, that a story exploits the narrative system on which it is based, transforming language into an image of itself, so that it signifies both what happened in the world and what that becomes in the artifice of the telling. In dialogic art one is properly engaged by the *immediate* impact of a speaker's words and demeanor of telling, what Bakhtin calls the individuality of intonation. Questions aroused by *what* the Mariner tells are focused by direct effects of his *telling*. And we as readers must react to the reactions of the Wedding Guest, when, for instance, he bursts out at one of the Mariner's pauses, "Why look'st thou so?" As is *not* the case with "Childe Roland," we as readers of "The Ancient Mariner" must confront the reaction of the Wedding Guest forced to confront directly something very strange, what appears less as simply a tale to be interpreted than as an experience of the incredible yet undeniable, therefore something *other*, that must interpret itself to him. There is, in other words, a doubling of the reciprocity within the poem as it is received by the reader, whose response is to the *effect* of the story as well as to the story told.

This enforcing of response to response by "The Ancient Mariner" assures that Coleridge's ballad means in a fashion quite different from the way "Childe Roland" means. The difference is illuminated by perhaps the best-known interpretation of "The Ancient Mariner," which nowadays is usually treated as a New Critical misreading: Robert Penn Warren's analysis of the poem as symbolizing processes of crime and punishment in a divinely ordered cosmos.[4] Warren unquestionably does misread so far as he treats Coleridge's poem as if it were Browning's, deciphering a hidden, latent pattern only implied by the poem's surface events. Warren assumes that within or beneath the Mariner's incredible narration is to be found an intelligible structure, a rationally describable system of coherence for events that otherwise would be only picturesque superstitiousness. Drawing on what he knows about Coleridge's religious beliefs, Warren deduces that the underlying coherence, without which the poem could not for him be a true work of art, to be a reaffirming of a divine orderliness of the cosmos. But *that* in the view of most subsequent critics is exactly what the poem represents as problematic.

Recent commentators tend to emphasize how the poem deploys elements of Christian belief confusingly, even contradictorily, just as the narrative evolution works against any simple cause-effect interpretations.[5] Thus the singling out of the Mariner because he kills the albatross is not easy to correlate with his singling out by Life-in-Death because of the chance of a dice throw. It was this point, in fact, that was stressed by E. E. Bostetter two decades ago in one of the first important challenges to Warren's reading.

> Critics are so accustomed to taking for granted the relentless logic of crime and punishment in the poem that they pass over without comment the astonishing implications of the dice game. Surely it knocks out any attempts to impose a systematic philosophic system, be it necessitarian, Christian, or Platonic on the poem . . . The total impression, then, which we get of the universe in *The Rime* is of unpredictable despotic forces . . . Within this context the Mariner's pious moral becomes inescapably ironic.[6]

Bostetter's anticipation of subsequent critiques of Warren justifies a brief consideration of a problem of critical method, a problem that, in fact, can be linked to assumptions about human psychology that have done much in our century to make fantasy a minor form. The most revealing symptom of what in Warren's reading bothers later critics is his treatment of the gloss as reliable, even though he was well aware it was added two decades after the original composition of the poem, and even though he notes imperfections in it, "the gloss should have made the poem clearer" (SE, 262), and "apparently the Gloss needs a gloss" (SE, 231). But all Warren's other observations represent the gloss's comments as unqualifiedly correct, and he consistently relies on it as corroborative of his reading, for example:

> The Gloss points to the important thing here: "He despiseth the creatures of the calm" (SE, 232) [though the verse does not tell us the Mariner *despises* the creatures]; "the gloss here [Part 4] tells us all we need to know" (SE, 246); "As the Gloss explains . . ."; "the Gloss tells us . . . (SE, 246); "since the Gloss has earlier dismissed the Polar Spirit . . . it seems more reasonable to me to . . ." (SE, 249–50)[7]

Warren's surprising blindness to the gloss as a possibly inadequate or uncertain interpretation of the poem in good part derives from his assurance that an interpretation can be definitively accurate, a deep meaning will explain surface structure. Contributing is Warren's refusal to face what Arac calls "the problem of religion," an "incoherence" in Coleridge's Christianity, which had drawn attack by Babbitt even before Warren wrote, and drew comments from Empson, Bostetter, and others after him. Babbitt's unqualified condemnation of the poem's "sham moral" vividly poses this problem of religion.

> The mode in which the Mariner is relieved of the burden of his transgression, symbolized by the albatross hung about his neck—namely, by admiring the color of water snakes—is an extreme example of the confusion to which I have already alluded: he obtains subrationally and unconsciously . . . the equivalent of Christian charity. . . . [T]he poem thus lays claim to a religious seriousness that at bottom it does not possess.[8]

Subsequent commentators have found it inconceivable, both on the basis of the poem itself and of what we know of Coleridge's interest in theology, that he was unaware of the problems posed to Babbittish conventionalized Christian piety by the Mariner's wanton act. The poem seems to most readers now to be *about* this problem, even though the gloss does its best to cover up such difficulties, to enforce on the rime a conventional moral respectability which, as Babbitt complains, the ballad itself does not justify. This discrepancy between gloss and rime throws into high relief the dubiety of any kind of systematically moralistic interpretation, whether it be Christian or the New Criticism's orthodoxy of organic form, or even a nihilistically existentialist one like Bostetter's. At issue in the ballad is the *question* of what may be meant by *blessing*, by a *curse*, what is the meaning of *crime*, what is *guilt*.

Warren's New Critical, essentially structuralist, imposition of meaningful form on the Mariner's puzzling rime is exactly analogous to the gloss's imposition on it of one kind of conven-

tionally pious reading. And both echo the Mariner's shipmates
within the poem, who interpret the killing of the albatross:

> For all averred, I had killed the bird
> That made the breeze to blow.
> Ah wretch! said they, the bird to slay,
> That made the breeze to blow (93–96)

and then reinterpret the act:

> Then all averred, I had killed the bird
> That brought the fog and mist.
> 'Twas right, said they, such birds to slay,
> That bring the fog and mist. (99–103)

The inconsistency of their interpretations not only suggests the
inadequacy of their superstition, but perhaps of all explanatory
readings of what is genuinely supernatural. As Jonathan Culler
suggests,

> the most interesting cases of fantasy are . . . those
> which force us to move yet another step up the ladder of
> self-consciousness by calling the assumption that litera-
> ture is always mimetic [into] question and preventing us
> from constructing fictional worlds.[9]

Even the final moral the Mariner articulates, *his* interpretation, fails in that it may not be wrong but it certainly oversimpli-
fies what he has told and the impact of his telling. Much of the
powerful effect of his telling first on the Wedding Guest and then
on us, the readers of his telling, derives from its refusal definitively to define, to summarize, to structure the meaning of what
happens, as his shipmates, the gloss, and Warren do summarize
for us the precise meaning of what has happened. Just as the
Mariner appears not to know why those he must teach are so
singled out, although he is sure his tale will be significant, he
cannot really explain why. A genuinely supernatural experience
is not going to be explicable in terms that constitute a satisfying
explanation to a contemporary critical intelligence. Yet, as the
Mariner dramatizes through his homely moral tag, because we
are human we are bound to try to explain such events. Yet what

we are really taught by the moral in context is the lesson of the Mariner's essential humility. He has his moral, but he appends it modestly to the end of long story, that depends very little on it. The powerful effect is created by the story itself, the spell it casts. Which bring us back to what I've termed its deceptive form.

It seems to me that the importance of that form, which we now term dialogic, is one of the things Coleridge calls attention to in his notorious remark to Mrs. Barbauld, part of which I've already cited.

> Mrs. Barbauld once told me that she admired the Ancient Mariner very much, but that there were two faults in it,—it was improbable, and had no moral. As for the probability, I owned that that might admit some question; but as to the want of moral, I told her that in my own judgement the poem had too much; and that the only, or chief fault, if I might say so, was the obtrusion of the moral sentiment so openly on the reader as a principal cause of action in a work of such pure imagination. It ought to have had no more moral than the *Arabian Nights'* tale of the merchant's sitting down to eat dates by the side of a well, and throwing the shells aside, and lo! a genie starts up, and says he *must* kill the aforesaid merchant *because* one of the date shells had, it seems, put out the eye of the genie's son.[10]

One thing this comment in its entirety suggests is that in an imaginative story the meaning lies *in* the story, not in some truth extractable from it. To say this is not to say that the story is meaningless, but that it is going to produce only a certain kind of meaning—namely, narrative meaning. The objection to a reading such as Warren's is that it produces a nonnarrative meaning, which is why it seems statically one-dimensional. It does not seem to take into sufficient account how much of Coleridge's poem fascinates us by the narrative dynamism with which it continually upsets its own orderings, breaks in upon itself so as to baffle not merely our expectations when we first read it, but, far more significantly, the understanding we have constructed from having read it when we *return* to the poem. A critic like Warren in essence explains by defining a single relation between surface phenomena of the poem and some deep pattern, the latter alone being determinative. But a dialogic work such as "The Ancient Mariner" is constituted by a continuous shifting of its depths and surfaces,[11] the complexity of whose changing interrelations both determines and is determined by the reader's continuously self-readjusting responses. Thematically this is illustrated by the Mariner's shipmates' superstitiousness. When we first read the poem we are likely to be struck by the discrepancy between their inverted interpretations of the Mariner's act. When we reread, knowing of the inversion to come, their original interpretation is for us already problematic. Analogously, knowing the nature of the Mariner's return profoundly complicates the way we respond to his description of his departure, without necessarily making us any more sure of the significance of his going forth, and his return.

Formally, as I have already suggested, "The Ancient Mariner's narrative surface becomes depth as Coleridge's artistry renders dubious the balladic simplicity his work seems to reproduce. This self-imagining, and therefore self-questioning, artistry's effects we appreciate more on each rereading. Thus the temporal movement of the ballad is not merely the advance of its narrative but also the progress of the poem in our consciousness of it, outside the time within the text. This extratextual progress is spectacularly dramatized by Coleridge's late addition of the gloss, with its superimposition of another temporal perspective on the original narrative, one not in the poem we read but not outside it either, since once it has been added we must read the poem through it. What the gloss especially dramatizes for us is both the human compulsion to interpret, to seek a pattern of meaning within a puzzling sequence of events, and the dangerous misapprehensions resulting from such interpreting. The gloss, then, is a complex means (Coleridge is driven to complex techniques because he writes for a literate audience committed to rational interpreting) for enforcing our attention, and enabling us to respond, to something like a told story, to be fascinated by something like the spell of a telling. This is another reason we don't suspect the Mariner as we do suspect Roland. We must accept the Mariner's tale because so indubitably the sailor casts a spell on the Wedding Guest. In what sense, one might say, can one challenge the truth of a story so potent? To respond to the poem at all a reader has to accept the actuality of this spell, the incantation that is the true rime of the Mariner. And this is why the poem means as story, not as a sugarcoated device for preaching a sermon on, let us say, "One Life." As Coleridge's title tells us, it is the rime that matters most.

We find the Mariner persuasive also because he so unhesitatingly assumes he is responsible for his nightmare. But it is doubtful how much that is an independent judgment and how much a conventional one he has internalized. He seems relieved when his shipmates praise him for killing the albatross and feels guilty when they condemn the act. And he patently believes he can convey to another how important is what has befallen him, even though in himself he is an unimportant person. His spellbinding power lies in his persuasion that there is significance for another in hearing what has happened to him, that his weird story is worth telling. It is worth telling, to be sure, because telling gives him temporary respite from his agony, but he is also convinced that it will benefit his listener, even though his capacity to define the nature of the benefit is limited.

Babbitt may be right that the Mariner's moral is a sham, or Bostetter that it is ironic, but the Mariner believes his story is one the Wedding Guest should hear. And the poem's narrator validates the Mariner's view when he reports that the guest was made by the story a "sadder and wiser man." This does not necessarily mean that the guest was affected by the Mariner's moral, but that the entire telling had profound impact on him— as it continues to have on us. The meaning of the poem for us reading it today, too, is inseparable from its telling, which is our hearing of it. What I've called the superficiality of the ballad results from our receiving it as a performance. It is meaningful as the telling of a story. When we hear a great cellist perform Bach, it is no denigration of the profundity of Bach's music when we say that what moves us now is this performance. It is this immediacy of execution, a primary characteristic of what nowadays we term dialogic experience, an engagement of performer and audience, out of which the significance of Coleridge's poem arises. Yet, obviously, our experience is not identical with that of the Wedding Guest—indeed, we experience his response as well as the Mariner's telling. So what does immediacy mean when applied to a literary text? Principally a self-reflexivity of form and language, a use of words that continually forces us to admit verbal and narrative self-complications, to see not only the events narrated but even the words of narration not as simple, transparent referents to something other than themselves. The words of narrative art are not mere carriers of the events, do not merely refer to the events of the story, but are constitutive—and complicative—of what happens in it.

For this reason Arden Reed's emphasis on rime as functioning in Coleridge's poem both as frozen mist and as ballad speaks exactly to the magic of Coleridge's performative telling,[12] as does Arac's citing of the accumulating self-created meanings of cross in the poem. What I've called the immediacy of "The Ancient Mariner" can be described as a consequence of the poet's composing a written text in a way equivalent to (though in fact different from) an orally performed ballad—the difference being expressive of Coleridge's insight into what an ordinary popular ballad conceals, this permitting his work a depth of impact on sophisticated or learned audiences that could not in them be aroused by a true ballad.

So far as post-Renaissance humanizing of the world was carried out through the growth of industrialized, technologically depersonalizing mass culture, basically performative modes of literature such as the ballad were pushed aside—so much so that by the early twentieth century, literary criticism virtually ignored problems of audience. Romantic poets, caught in the first surge of this movement, tried to retain an equivalent to the reciprocal, ostensive qualities of literature in its performative modes. The chief stylistic endeavors of both Wordsworth and Byron were directed to this task. The fantasies of Coleridge and Keats are part of the same effort. But one can understand that, given the strength of the trends they were resisting, for Romantic poets fantasy could not have seemed an efficacious means, so there is relatively little Romantic poetry in this mode. And what little was created had to be characterized by seemingly transparent yet in fact intricately self-conscious artistry such as we find in "The Ancient Mariner." For in the early nineteenth century only in this fashion could anything like a vital interplay between artwork and audience be valorized with supernatural subject matter. This is a major source of the subversiveness of fantasy, which as yet has been little recognized, but which provides important revelations about the strongest tendencies of modern soceity to exclude and exorcise whatever is neither natural nor amenable to rational explanation.

FREUD'S FANTASTIC STORY

Romantic fantasy strives to recover qualities analogous to those important to performative literary art. As it is about others, so fantasy seeks provocative even oppositional interplay between work and audience. Fantasy, that is to say, presumes a heterogenous *discourse situation*. It links human beings in a cosmos perceived as containing something other than humankind, and the audience response it evokes is predicated on an assumption of a human solidarity composed of heterogeneity, not homogeneity, just as Mariner and Wedding Guest are very different people coming from and going on to very different lives. With the spread of rationalized industrialized systems around the globe, the value for the diversity from which fantasy derives and to which it appeals has been replaced by antithetical assumptions about the nature of human solidarity. These find powerful intellectual expression in structuralist modes of thinking which underlie our century's dominant philosophies, anthropologies, and psychologies. In our century, to cite a pertinent instance, a vast variety of different non-Western peoples have been lumped together by Westerners as "primitive." As Levi-Strauss, indiscriminately mingling myths from widely diverse cultures, can speak confidently of "*the* savage mind," so Freud—who works as consistently as Levi-Strauss from a concept of binary oppositions, though recognizing but a single, primal one, the sexual—regularly speaks as if all preliterate people were essentially alike, referring for instance to "*the* old, animistic concept." The simultaneous popularization

by scientists like Lévy-Bruhl of "the primitive mind" and "primitive art" by artists such as Picasso at the turn of the century
suggests how fundamental to modern Western culture is this new
concept of the primitive. The origins of it are traceable to
Rousseauvian Romanticism's admiration for natural freedom
and harmony with natural processes. But by the end of the
nineteenth century celebratory attitudes had given way to fear of
the primitive as dangerously elemental, ferocious, unbridled, a
force to be controlled if possible rather than to be enjoyed, and, if
difficult to control, to be exterminated. Inevitably the concept of
the primitive had become contaminated with racist and imperial-
ist implications. For Picasso and Freud equally, interest in the
primitive expresses not concern with what is other in itself but
the other as mere instrument for revealing truth about what to
them is genuinely important, modern, Westernized man.

As total humanizing means dismissal of significant otherness, so the differences between humankind's internal otherness
is also done away with. *Good* and *normal* cannot now be
conceived in terms of heterogeneity; primitive elements in society or the mind are either to be eliminated or matured (forcibly if
necessary) into conformity with the adult, modern, Western
European model (usually male) for all humanity. In these
conditions, literary fantasy can exist only marginally or in disguise. The themes of loneliness and isolation in "The Ancient
Mariner" are premonitory of the precarious existence of the
fantastic mode in the twentieth century, but even more ominously predictive is the epithet applied to the Mariner in the
poem: "loon." Fantasy is about to be defined as pathology.

The evolutionary direction defined by differences between
Coleridge's dialogic fantasy and Browning's dramatic monologue, therefore, is fully realized by Freud's essay on "The Uncanny." Here Freud explains a Romantic fantastic tale, E. T. A.
Hoffmann's "Sandman," as a delusion of personal psychology;
the fantastic is thus explained away by an improvement in
psychology. "Many things in Hoffmann's story," Freud assures
us, "seem arbitrary and meaningless so long as we deny all
connection between fears about the eye and castration; but they
become intelligible as soon as we replace the Sandman by the

dreaded father at whose hands castration is awaited" (F, 37). A story that seemed incomprehensible, in fact is perfectly intelligible to the psychologically enlightened. There is no Sandman; he is a delusionary symptom of a primitive human fear.[13]

Freudian psychology is a major force in the modern humanizing of the world. What so often had appeared mysterious, a manifestation of unknown powers, the strange effects of something other, through this new psychology can be scientifically demonstrated to derive from rationally describable causes entirely within the human psyche. The power of Freud's assertions needs no confirmation today, and their popularity helps to explain why in our century there have been few useful studies of fantasy. Modern critiques read through its weirdness to find some real principle of universal structure beneath the illusory appearance of singularity. This is how Freud explains away the uncanny in Hoffmann's story. Yet if one looks to Freud's practice in "The Uncanny" (to which most recent critiques of fantasy have been indebted), one finds the essay to be logically confused to the point of incoherence. This is not to denigrate Freud's accomplishment, but to suggest that the value of examining carefully the foundations on which his claim to write a scientific treatise rests. In the rhetoric of this claim to be able to do away with primitive fantasies one sees plainly the link between Western scientific thought and imperialism, between enlightened thinking and humanism as the extirpation of otherness. For the identification of primitive features in the psyche "is a central mode of reincorporation of the other," a subtler "form of conquest" that serves as "its displacement, its disguise, even its excuse."[14] Freud's remarkable integrity in developing a particular conception, however unsavory and upsetting it might be, carries him beyond the limits of scientific self-skepticism and logicality (what D'Arcy McNickle, a "primitive" Indian who became a respected scientist, called "exacting, unexhibitionary description") to gain for him the power of enormous popular influence. If one wishes to understand the effect of "The Uncanny" on critics, it is necessary to recognize that its source is precisely its concealed betrayal of scientific logicality. Cixous observes that "The Uncanny," while pretending to be a piece of logical exposition, becomes itself a kind of fantastic tale. Freud must write what Cixous calls a "strange novel" (Cixous, 525), must undermine the logic of rigorous scientific analysis, to create something far more thrilling, because what he claims to prove is nothing else than the premise from which he launches his argument, namely that there exists no such thing as fantastic experience, only illusions of it.

Freud's fundamental assumption is that nothing can happen that is not naturalistically explicable. This is a reasonable opinion, and one widely held, but if one is trying to demonstrate that belief in the supernatural is foolish, it is the assumption that needs to be proved. Exactly what Freud does not address in "The Uncanny" is his conception of the real, the possible, the scientifically naturalistic, just as in defining the fantastic, Todorov, among others who follow Freud closely, assumes that what is natural is plainly and universally understood, that only what is called supernatural needs to be analyzed because only it is problematic—even though Raymond Williams had already demonstrated that few words have been used in more different ways than *natural*. Even so, Freud's assumption is perhaps more surprising, because he begins making much of what might be called the self-contradictions of language, of how the apparently simple and commonplace German word *heimlich* has come to possess two antithetic meanings, "familiar," and "strange" or "secret" and "dangerous," that is, *unheimlich*. Freud explains the terror of *unheimlich* experience by postulating a principle of the human psyche to repetition-compulsion. Whatever one encounters that activates the postulated repetition-compulsion mechanism will be perceived—unless the experiencer has mastered Freud's psychology—as uncanny, a return of what seems alien but in fact is rooted within us. So Freud observes, "the uncanny is in reality nothing new or foreign"—in his view there can be no otherness—"but something familiar and old-established in the mind that has been estranged by repression" (F, 47). What, however, is the reality to which Freud refers? So far as one can determine from the essay, reality for Freud is what is not delusional. Because it so illuminates the difficulties that have beset interpretations of literary fantasy in our time, it will be worthwhile to sketch briefly how this circular logic leads Freud into what Blake called "multiplication of divisions," a proliferating sequence of distinctions that finally must be abandoned arbitrarily, lest the fundamental premise of a unitary, universal principle be exposed as convenient fiction, or, to keep to Freud's language, an expedient postulate.

Freud attributes the uncanny effect of Hoffmann's story "The Sandman" to its evocation in the reader of repressed, infantile fears of castration (F, 35–37). The relation of "uncanny effect" to "infantile psychology" Freud explains by deciding

> to postulate the principle of repetition-compulsion in the unconscious mind, based upon instinctual activity and probably inherent in the very nature of the instincts—a principle powerful enough to overrule the pleasure principle . . . whatever reminds us of this inner *repetition-compulsion* is perceived as uncanny. F, 44).

But almost immediately Freud adds to this speculation about a principle more powerful than his earlier postulated pleasure principle a quite different impulse. He asserts that there also persist in all of "us"

> the old, animistic concept of the universe, which was characterized by the idea that the world was peopled with the spirits of human beings, and by the narcissistic overestimation of subjective mental processes (such as the belief in the omnipotence of thoughts) . . . as well as by all those other figments of the imagination with which man, in the unrestricted narcissim of that stage of development, strove to withstand the inexorable laws of reality . . . everything which now strikes us as "uncanny" fulfills the condition of stirring those vestiges of animistic mental activity. (F, 46)

If we are to believe Freud's claim that everything that seems uncanny derives from these vestiges, we would expect him to link the "old animistic concept" to activation of his postulated repetition-compulsion principle. Freud makes no such link, covering this evasion by asserting correspondence between the infantile psychology of the individual and the infantile condition of mankind. This linking is further emphasized in *Totem and*

Taboo: Resemblances Between Psychic Lives in Savages and Neurotics (1912), where the subtitle reveals how little interest Freud has in other peoples, except as instrument, so far as they may help to reveal characteristics of adult, modern, Western man. The unneurotic European adult will not, and should not, take seriously uncanny experiences, as less advanced (infantile) peoples must, because the European can recognize these as delusory phenomena rooted in primitive conditions that can and should be "surmounted," to use one of Freud's favorite, if slippery, locutions in this essay.

Throughout Freud's descriptions of uncanny effects, he assumes an absolute antithesis between the real and the imagined. Thus: "an uncanny effect is often and easily produced by effacing the distinction between imagination and reality" (F, 50). Yet, as Freud recognizes, this raises the problem that his proposition that the uncanny "is nothing else than a hidden, familiar thing that has undergone repression and then emerged from it" is "clearly not convertible," because obviously "not everything that fulfills this condition . . . is uncanny" (F, 51). Freud's solution to this difficulty is to create still another distinction, this time between "the uncanny that is actually experienced" and the uncanny "as we merely picture it or read about it" in "fiction and literary productions" (F, 53). He goes on to say, rather surprisingly, that "the actual occurrence of uncanny feelings" in "real life" is connected for the most part to vestiges in us of beliefs from "our primitive forefathers" in the "omnipotence of thoughts, instantaneous wish-fulfillments, secret power to harm and the like." These beliefs "nowadays . . . we have *surmounted* [Freud's emphasis] . . . but we do not feel quite sure of our new set of beliefs." For as soon as something

> actually happens in our lives which seems to support the old discarded beliefs, we get a feeling of the uncanny; . . . 'So, after all, it is true that one can kill a person by merely desiring his death,' and so on. And, conversely, he who has completely and finally dispelled animistic beliefs in himself, will be insensible to this type of the uncanny. (F, 54)

The uncanny effects more common in literature than in actual life are, Freud asserts, those created by "a return of repressed material, not a removal of *belief* in its objective reality" (F, 55), even though this assertion leads inevitably to the seeming paradoxes that

> in the first place a great deal that is not uncanny in fiction would be so if it happened in real life; and in the second place that there are many more means of creating uncanny effects in fiction than there are in real life. (F, 56)

The first paradox Freud explains by claiming that when we read literature such as fairy tales, "the world of reality is left behind," and when Dante or Shakespeare create settings that "differ from the real world by admitting superior spiritual entities . . . so long as they remain within their setting of poetic reality their usual attributes of uncanniness fail to attach to such beings. . . . We order our judgment to the imaginary reality imposed on us by the writer" (F, 57). Genuinely uncanny effects in literature, therefore, only occur when "the writer pretends to move in the world of common reality" and accepts "all the conditions operating to reduce uncanny feelings in real life; and everything that would have an uncanny effect in reality has it in his story" (F, 57). This might seem to blur the distinction between fiction and real life Freud has insisted upon, but more important is the fact that the uncanny in literature with which he is concerned is thus dwindled down to work by writers following nineteenth-century conventions of realism or naturalism. Such a writer "takes advantage . . . of our supposed surmounted superstitiousness; he deceives us into thinking that he is giving us the sober truth, and then after all oversteps the bounds of possibility. We react to his inventions as we should have reacted to real experiences; by the time we have seen through his trick it is already too late and the author has achieved his object" (F, 57–58). This provocation of uncanny effects does indeed seem cheap and spurious, and Freud remarks that "we retain a feeling of dissatisfaction, a kind of grudge against the attempted deceit," which, he insists, belongs "only to that class of the uncanny which proceeds from forms of thought that have been surmounted" (F, 58).

Surely this kind of uncanny literature is not of much interest, and one expects Freud to return to the "other class" of the uncanny more common in literature "which proceeds from repressed complexes." But all he says of this is that it is "more irrefragable and remains as powerful in fiction as in real experience [wherein, one recalls, the uncanny is more commonly linked to surmounted beliefs] except in one point" (F, 58). One regrets that Freud did not elucidate this point, but one should not be surprised at the omission. That his logical conclusion should be disappointing and arbitrary is inevitable, because, under the guise of orderly analysis and systematic argument he only ingeniously and interestingly reasserts his original, unanalyzed premise. This failure in no way weakens the reassuring effect of the essay for those who share his desire to do away with the fantastic as a symptom of exploded superstitiousness and primitive fear. And during this century these have become just about everyone, especially literary critics. This is why there has been so little illumination of the more problematic features of literary fantasy. To deal with these one needs a different psychological approach, a different set of hypotheses about psychic activity, a more dynamically open-minded interest in superstition. To conceive what might be involved in such a psychology, we do best to turn back to poets who entertained the possibility of creating fantasy in a world without superstition or magic. In so doing, moreover, we can illustrate that fantasy may be a less narrow topic than it at first appears. When we examine the implications for psychological capability exhibited in Keats's "Ode to Psyche," for example, we can perceive one basis for some artists' resistance to dominating conceptions of literature as inherently realistic, as successful only when unreservedly mimetic. Attention to fantasy encourages awareness that in a subtler fashion than Soviet Socialist Realism, which the modern Russian writer Abram Tertz (Andrei Sinyavsky) declared made fantasy the only realism possible for an honest Soviet writer, one function of nineteenth- and twentieth-century aesthetic realism was to conceal certain possible truths about the nature and limitations of the reality so represented.

CHAPTER SIX

Self-Enchantment

How on earth can a man have the nerve to pose as an expert
on religion when he actually believes in God?

KAREL ČAPEK, *The Absolute at Large*

HE PSYCHOLOGY MAKING POSSIBLE THE CREATION
of Romantic fantasy is illuminated with pecu-
liar brilliance by Keats's "Ode to Psyche," even
though this ode is usually treated, not unjustly, as inferior to those addressing the urn,
the nightingale, and melancholy. But we may
conjecture that the later odes were to a de-
gree made possible by "Psyche," as it, in turn, may owe something to the successful composition of "La Belle Dame" just a
week earlier.[1] Keats said of the Psyche ode that it was the first
poem over which he had taken "moderate pains." Exactly what
the pains entailed we do not know, but their origin may be
suggested by the ode's representation of how the poet's mind was
aroused by its own creative self-consciousness to admit into itself a reality of otherness grounded in no external phenomena.
It is this paradoxical activity, a realizing of something other
than oneself though self-reflection, that is fundamental to the
unFreudian psychology on which Romantic fantasizing depends.

FANTASTIC APULEIUS

Although commentators on the "Ode to Psyche" regularly observe that Keats's primary source was Apuleius' novel, or romance, *Metamorphoses*, usually known as *The Golden Ass*, none,

so far as I can determine, has discussed at length the unusual qualities of that source. In Apuleius' masterpiece the Cupid-Psyche story is presented as a pretty piece of nonsense told by a crazed crone to cheer a despairing girl who has been kidnapped by robbers.[2] Scarcely is the tale concluded than the robbers are massacred and the girl freed, only to see her lover then treacherously slain by a jealous rival. She successfully plots the murder of this killer, after which she takes her own life. If Keats ignored this context, it is possible that subconsciously at least he may have been affected by the whole of Apuleius' work, not just the inset Cupid-Psyche tale. Even if such a speculation is misguided, the mixture of parallelism and contrast between Apuleius' art and Keats's gives unusual insight into creative processes central to fantasy.

Apuleius wrote about A.D. 150 when, according to the celebrated opening of Gibbon's *Decline and Fall*, the Roman Empire was at the height of a period of unexampled peace, prosperity, and graceful civilization. *The Golden Ass*, however, opens with a story of how a man, significantly named Socrates, is murdered by a witch who runs a disreputable tavern.

> She laid Socrates' head over on one side, and drove the sword into the left part of his throat up to the hilt, and caught the spout of blood in a leathern bottle which she held ready, so carefully that not a single drop was left visible. . . . I saw Meroe . . . thrust her hand down through the wound into the very entrails, and, after groping about, finally wrench out the heart of my unhappy comrade. And he, with his gullet slit by the impact of the blade, uttered a cry through the wound (or rather a gurgle,) and burbled out his ghost. (A, 40)

In the morning, amazingly, Socrates rises as if normal and continues his journey with his friend, later lying down to drink from a stream.

> But he had no sooner touched the dewy sparkle of the water with his lips, when the wound in his throat gaped open wide, and the sponge suddenly sprang out, a little

gush of blood accompanying it. And his body now void
of life, would have collapsed into the stream had I not
gripped him by the leg and with difficulty dragged him
higher up the bank . . . and then buried him in the
sandy soil . . .
That done, trembling, terrified, I rode through many
strange and desert places, as if driven by the guilt of a
murder. I abandoned my country and home. (A, 44)

From this horrendous opening, which in the romance is
treated as a "light, gay tale," we advance to the center of the
narrative, how the protagonist Lucius' foolish curiosity about
magic leads him to be transformed into an ass. In asinine form he
undergoes harrowing misadventures involving sadistic lust, rob-
bery, mutilation, and torture in a society wherein brute power is
the sole authority. Apuleius' romance is, in fact, a superb
example of what Bakhtin calls menippea, absolutely unprettified
and unsentimentalized and even unmitigated by Rabelesian good
humor, though Apuleius' story overflows with bawdry and scato-
logical jokes. What retransforms Lucius into a man, providing
him for the first time with a worthy purpose in life, is a blessing
bestowed by the goddess Isis. Apuleius' protagonist is redeemed
from the brutality of sensual existence and victimizing by black
magic through worship of a foreign goddess well outside the
traditional Olympian pantheon.

The "Ode to Psyche" may subtly reflect something of
Apuleius' unorthodox spirituality triumphing over the carnivalesque brutality of Roman high civilization. For Keats's worship is of
the pagan Psyche, "too late for antique vows." It is noteworthy
that the traditional Greco-Roman gods and goddesses appear in
no flattering light in *The Golden Ass*. Venus is represented as
insanely jealous of the mortal Psyche's beauty. Ceres and Juno
refuse to intercede for the girl, even though they recognize how
unfairly she is treated. When she prays to Juno, for example, the
queen of the gods, much revered in Rome, replies

By my old faith . . . I would that I could lend an ear to
your request. But propriety will not permit me to run
counter to the wishes of Venus, my daughter-in-law,

whom I have always cherished as my own child. Besides, I must not forget the Laws which forbid the
entertainment of fugitive slaves against the inclination
of their owners. (A, 131)

This parody of Roman legalizing morality is reinforced by
other sardonic comments, as when Jove assures good attendance
at an Assembly of the Gods by imposing a monetary fine on
absentees (A, 141). In both *The Golden Ass* and the "Ode to
Psyche" official religion is not a source of genuine spiritual
experience. As Apuleius' hero turns to an Egyptian divinity, so
Keats turns to an ignored, belated pagan half-goddess. Whether
or not Apuleius' satire of conventional religion in any way
encouraged Keats, one must be impressed by the pagan women,
not men it is well worth noticing, possessed of supernatural
powers in his late works, including La Belle Dame, Moneta, and
Lamia. But in at least one respect these strangely marginalized
feminine figures of weird power are radically different from
Apuleius' Isis, who acts for Lucius as redemptress. Keats's later
goddesses are ambiguous supernaturals whose effects for good or
ill on mortals are uncertain, just as the religious status of the
poet's "self-created" Psyche is profoundly dubious. This difference from Apuleius reflects the increased skepticism of the
cultural situation within which Keats wrote, an ambiance demanding that any evocation of supernaturalism begin where it
does in the "Ode to Psyche," in the problematics of self-
enchantment.

FANTASY'S STYLISTIC INVOLUTION

It is not inconceivable that Keats found some inspiration even
from the style of *The Golden Ass* (which he knew in Aldington's
translation). Although Apuleius' principal subject is the brutal
actualities of life under a decaying but still savagely exploitive
imperialism, his manner is spectacularly ornate, a dazzling
display of self-conscious rhetorical inventiveness. Although no
English translator before Lindsay has done justice to the artifices
of Apuleius, even the dullest translators have not been able
entirely to conceal them. The preface is representative.

In this Milesian Tale, reader, I shall string together a medley of stories, and titillate your agreeable ears with a merrily whispered narrative, if you will not refuse to scan this Egyptian paper written and a subtle pen of Nilotic reeds. It tells how the forms and fortunes of men were converted into alien natures, and then back again by the twist of fate into their first selves. Read and wonder; but first I shall answer your query: Who is this man? (A, 31)

And at least one passage in the romance seems specifically germane to Keats's ode, in which, to be sure, Apuleius' fantastic anthropologizing is transformed into a thematically significant inversion. When in the romance Psyche raises the lamp to discover the man she has engaged herself to kill is a beautiful god:

At the sight of him the flame burned cheerfully higher, and the razor dulled its sacriligious edge.

But, as for Psyche, she was terrified at the sight. She lost all self-control; and swooning, pallid, trembling she dropped to her knees and sought to hide the knife—deep in her own bosom. And so she would have done, had it not been that the blade, shrinking from such an atrocity, fell to the floor out of her heedless hands.

And then, for all her faintness and fear, she felt her flagging spirits revive as she gazed at the beauty of the god's face. (A, 121–22)

Then after the fatal event, the drop of burning oil falling on the shoulder of the sleeping god, we are given this apostrophe:

O bold and reckless lamp! base officer of love! to burn the very god of Flame—you that some lover, inspired by the need to possess the beloved even at night, first devised. (A, 122)

This passage could have contributed to Keats's reversing of the traditional story, by which he makes the lamp a beacon of love rather than the instrument separating Cupid and Psyche, an illumination drawing love in instead of driving love out. Whether or not the inversion was encouraged by Apuleius' elaborate rhetoric, Keats's poem manifests a significant enhancement of the consistently paradoxical relation between Apuleius' subject and his extraordinary artifices of linguistic virtuosity. Lindsay's example of his fundamental method is as apt as any—a phrase about the girl who delays suicide only so she can revenge her murdered lover: *invita remansit in vita,* which I translate as "unwillingly she sustains the will to live." In the "Ode to Psyche" Keats intensifies this kind of rhetorical play to rework the Cupid-Psyche story that had attracted him since the writing of "Sleep and Poetry," and in so reworking he establishes the basis for his maturest poetic accomplishments.[3]

Overtly self-conscious art deployed in the exhibition of experiences conventionally characterized as realistic and magical might best describe Apuleius' work. Through rhetorical virtuosity, moreover, he succeeds in representing matter that had normally been excluded from the mainstream of classical literature, including unsparingly savage representations of civilized violence of slum naturalism and, on the other side, describing an authentic personal religious conversion. In the "Ode to Psyche" Keats goes beyond Apuleius in exploring the power of his own inventive imagination. This leads him into a more complicated relation to his literary heritage and to more radical testings of capabilities of his language. Unlike Apuleius, Keats employs a deceptively simple-seeming rhetoric distinguished by unostentatious diction and an easy flowing syntax. These qualities form a deceitful surface so far as the poem works to bring out the intrinsically self-challenging qualities of his words. Keats taps into the self-contradictory energies that are the essential life of verbal discourse, on which depend its capability to expand and evolve. These energies, of course, we normally ignore, just as we would dismiss as hallucinatory a vision of pagan deities embracing on a modern lawn. Keats demonstrates in his ode, however, that by exploiting the self-inverting potential inherent in language's polysemous qualities one may empower one's imagination to pass beyond the conventionally inscribed limits of what is imaginable as real. In the "Ode to Psyche" his words do not merely represent his imagining but are used to permit him to realize—in the literal sense of "make real"—a vision that would be delusory without such turning back on itself of his means of imaging, his language. Through this involuting of the poetic text within itself, Keats carries us beyond the normal antithesis between "to dream" and "to see" to delineate effective imagining as possessing and being possessed by a creative potency that unifies the normal opposition of "dreaming" and "seeing," that becomes a realization of the oxymoronic doubleness intrinsic to the word *vision:* to see and more than see.

THE SELF-INSPIRATION OF "PSYCHE"

When Keats begins his ode, "Surely I dreamt today, or did I see the winged Psyche with awakened eyes," he deliberately echoes a phrase from Spenser. Yet the phrase seems also consciously employed to provide the poet ground from which to query his "waking dream." The Spenserian locution authorizes, one might say, an imagining excluded by post-Spenserian systems of enlightened rationality. I assume, of course, that while out walking, perhaps on Hampstead Heath, Keats did not actually stumble over Cupid and Psyche, that he "invented" the encounter his poem describes. (The quotation marks around "invented" are there to remind the reader how complicated and ill-defined within criticism is the action referred to by that simple verb.) In a sense, the ode is about the meaning of poetic invention. This is why the speaker's question "did I?" directs all the involuting movements of the poem. In effect it poises us between regarding the poet's invention as mere daydreaming, as self-deluding, or as an awakening of himself to an actuality not accessible to a mind less capable of inventive imagining, as escaping from self-imposed limits of normal seeing. The poet begins with this uncertainty, because at issue throughout his poem is the oxymoron of an impossible sight. The seeing of what cannot be seen concretizes the act of the poet's skeptical intelligence fantasizing, creating psychically an imagined sensuality, relaxed yet totally fulfilled, of supernatural beings embraced, " 'mid hush'd cool-rooted flowers, fragrant-eyed," while their "lips touch'd not but had not bade adieu." The words evoking an incredible "lyrical remembrance of love past" inseparable from "suspenseful anticipation of love about to be appeased."[4] How, in every sense of that tricky little word, Keats asks, might I have perceived this love scene? He thereby opens the poem into an exploration of the human potential for imaginatively enriching, rather than delusorily falsifying, perceptions of reality.

Psyche, after all, is the "loveliest vision far / Of all Olympus' faded hierarchy" not only because in Apuleius' romance Psyche's loveliness is the cause of all her trouble, but also because Keats has imagined her: she is his "loveliest vision." Nor should one overlook here the parallel between the poet seeing the sleeping gods and Psyche's unlawful seeing of the sleeping Cupid, the sight which precipates her sufferings of separation. As Porphyro's singing of "La Belle Dame sans Merci" in "The Eve of St. Agnes" wakes Madeline from her dream of him to the reality of his presence where he does not belong, so the poet's ode must reawaken the goddess into a reality which is somehow spiritualized not by conventionalized religious sentiment but by a personal worship that the conventionally pious would condemn. Like Porphyro, the poet of the "Ode to Psyche" must authenticate a "religious admiration" blasphemous to the orthodox. Yet the protagonist of "The Eve of St. Agnes" belongs to an earlier time—"ages long ago"—when superstition flourished, while the poet of the ode must create by his song faith in a later time bereft of credulities in supernatural enrichings of ordinary reality.

Psyche can be so radiantly present, paradoxically, only because the poet recognizes her as belonging to what has faded, that her power is restorable only through his private envisioning of her. This is why a scholarly reader might accuse Keats of exaggerating Psyche's fadedness, for, of course, she had been much celebrated in the Renaissance and was a favorite among eighteenth-century classicizers. But such public conventionalized preservation had not truly revitalized her: in it she exists only allegorically, or metaphorically, part of a formal tradition substituting for an original genuine supersitious belief.[5] In herself, despite conventionalized references to her, Psyche is now invisible; only through something the poet does to his powers of perceiving can she be made to reappear, a process of reappearance in which she disappears for us, as in the progress of the poem she vanishes into the poet and becomes his mind.

"Too late for antique vows, Too, too late for the fond believing lyre," Psyche is "fluttering among the faint Olympians," the verb suggesting the marginality of her existence that the poet will recenter within himself. She gains potency, finally becoming the invisible energy of his mind, only through the poet's imaginative singing of seeing "by my own eyes inspired." Self-inspiration allows him to pray to become both her choir and choiric hymn, both singer and song, both worshipper and worship. He answers his own prayer by praying. In the final stanzas this fusion of agent with action is reinforced as Psyche becomes identified with his mind. Keats engages in worship of what he has quite consciously created, thereby yielding himself up to self-aroused inspiration.

It is not unreasonable, therefore, to call the Psyche ode narcissistic. But we may remember that originally Narcissus believed he saw someone else in the water, whereas Keats is from the first less innocent (even as he is more self-conscious than Pygmalion), singing Psyche's "secrets" into her "own soft-conched ear," deliberately admiring and adoring his reinvention, which has been reanimated by his adoration. Not surprisingly, the ode has been condemned as fanciful, as self-indulgent, and as unstrengthened by any relation to external actualities that play so active a role in both the odes to the urn and the nightingale. But self-indulgence is the point of "Psyche." The ode summons and addresses the creative potency within the poet's mind, and its success is to affirm the mind's power of self-enchanting. Of course, to most sensible and reasonable people, Keats merely deludes himself to the degree that he is serious about his vision. That is why he writes the poem as he does. In a society in which skepticism has triumphed, the possibility of enchantment can only begin in the privacy of self-enchantment.

The power Keats evokes in inventing Psyche is the power essential to Romantic fantasy. If, as has been suggested, the landscape described in the final stanza of the ode accords with what Keats had learned as a medical student about the physical configurations of his brain, that identity would be appropriate to

the poem's self-involuting.[6] For the ode strives to realize a power
in the mind to carry itself beyond what it has taught itself are its
delimiting conditions—a power that originates in intense reflec-
tion on itself and its fashionings. If, indeed, Keats uses the
physical structure of the brain, he does so not to define by
confining his imagination but to increase and improve what
imagination by transforming itself can accomplish. Finding some
"*untrodden* region of the mind," he will, he says, "dress" a "rosy
sanctuary" there with the "wreathed trellis" of a "working brain"
that is full of

> buds and bells, and stars without a name,
> With all the gardener Fancy e'er could feign,
> Who breeding flowers, will never breed the
>   same. (11.61–63)

Fancy, as more than one critic has observed, goes beyond natural
processes of breeding that produce sameness, even while that
gardener remains bound to the nature which his breedings feign.
But the key suggestion in these lines is that the brain is full, ready
to overflow, to go beyond known flowers and known stars. The
poet's fantasizing mind is pregnant, not least with Psyche-power.
This male poet's mind now embodies a feminine divinity. Keats's
reversing of the traditional Cupid-Psyche story, so that the bright
torch is a welcoming beacon to love rather than its destruction,
climactically epitomizes this sexual doubling as a prime source of
the poet's delight in the imagining-inventing of supernatural
sensual gratifications, "all soft delight / that shadowy thought
can win." The final image of the poem should be of love, no
longer merely "Cupid," from an outer darkness drawn into the
poet's illuminatively feminized mind, no longer a mere extrinsic
image, merely metaphoric "Psyche," but Keats's psyche.

   This internalizing may be seen as a solution to a problem
that underlies Apuleius' inset tale, what might be described as the
dangerous enthrallment of beauty, a theme surely fresh in
Keats's mind a week after composing "La Belle Dame." In *The
Golden Ass* Psyche's dazzling beauty brings her "no benefit." She
is admired "but only as men admire an exquisitely finished
statue," so that "she hated the beauty that gave pleasure to all the

world save herself" (A, 107). Were the poet to remain only a devout worshipper of the goddess external to him, he would be restrictively enchanted—enthralled—rather than empowered to enchant. And this is, in fact, the weakness of the younger Keats's poetry, which expresses only his enthrallment to wondrous beauty he imagines, a subjection to desire without performance. Just as Porphyro must enter Madeline to realize the magic of their love, so Psyche must enter the poet, empowered by him, empowering him.[7]

The feminizing of the poet's mind completes the deliberate narcissism in which the poem originates, intensifying his joy in what he can realize through imagination. By fancying he releases a feminineness within himself, and this released feminity he experiences as a joyous welcoming of masculinity, what he had before taken for granted as natural to him. Such androgynous consciousness attained through self-reflexivity epitomizes that self-enchantment in which Romantic fantasy must originate if the fantasist is to achieve the power to enchant others. Because fantasy in the rationalized, post-Enlightenment world seeks to recover otherness, some such radically transformative spell cast upon the self by the self is required fully to liberate the possibility of effective sharing of fantastic creations. And for the Romantics, only sharing, significance for the community as well as the artist's self, justifies imaginative adventuring.[8]

THE MAGIC IN OXYMORON

Only by admitting unconstrainedly—that is, by taking joy in— his power to fantasize can a post-Enlightenment poet hope to create a magicality analogous to that appearing more spontaneously in lifeways less skeptical and more credulous, that magicality less capable, however, of illuminating the full powers of the human imagination. By finding in language itself a means of self-enchanting, the Romantic poet becomes a kind of surpasser-successor to the traditional magician, for whom the practice of magic was a difficult discipline demanding special linguistic skills and capability for unusual mental concentration. The style of the Psyche ode, a style founded in oxymoron, is the result of an equivalent concentration aimed at bringing out the most deeply hidden—and dangerous—property in words, even—or especially—ordinary words, the self-controverting energy that allows them to change and to betray their established meanings, even to absolute reversals, so that *let* which meant "hinder" to Hamlet to us means "allow."

The effectiveness of Keats's concentration in the "Ode to Psyche," like the imposition of one lens over another increasing the power of light, constitutes a happy intensification of the awkward self-consciousness characterizing his early verse, in which aspiration consistently outpaces realization. In the Psyche ode Keats not only revises, reworks, and makes entirely his own a sterile piece of his literary culture, but also consistently, rather than sporadically, as in earlier poems, exploits the fundamentally catachretic qualities of language through which he accomplishes the feat of recovery. He does not employ the formal trope of oxymoron with extraordinary frequency (though the Psyche ode includes "tuneless numbers," "sweet enforcement," "glow-worm of the sky," "delicious moan," and "pleasant pain," to cite only obvious examples). It is what might be called the secondary and multiply intersecting effects resulting from his consistent awareness of self-contradiction as inherent in all words and phrases, conflicts which surface visibly in oxymoron, that constitutes the linguistic foundation of the ode's artistry. This, in turn, may be regarded as a foundation for all of Keats's best later poems, for the intensity of these works appears especially in the power of their diction and phrasing to articulate movingly contradictoriness of thought, feeling, and action. The great odes, "The Fall of Hyperion" and "Lamia," are constructed, both in their verbal details and in their rhetorical structures and thematic developments, upon the evocation of fiercely dynamic impasses within a seemingly cool, calm classicism: "Thou still unravished bride of quietness," for instance. The basis of this productively conflicted quality within serenity is first given shape in the "Ode to Psyche" through its self-inspired creation of a supernatural energy within the imagining poet.

Before the Romantic era the trope of oxymoron had most frequently prevailed in religious poetry, possibly for the reason

Coleridge noted, that in religious language words "convey all their separate meanings at once, no matter how incomprehensible or absurd the *collective* meaning may be."[9] For a skeptical, post-Napoleonic poet, however, anything supernatural was fantastic. Effects of supernatural experience could be evoked, consequently, only through language deliberately making use of oxymoron in a newly complex fashion, conceiving of it as a potentiality intrinsic to all language, even the simplest and most commonplace as well as to the most private. The later poet attempting the supernatural must create without any appeal to or support from a shared faith. Romantic fantasy, therefore, displays miracles without either recognized religious bases or implications.

What I've termed Keats's antipathy to Wordsworthian naturalism can be regarded as a risky extending or developing of the older poet's argument for poetry written in "a selection of the language really used by men." Like Wordsworth, Keats perceives words to be awesome powers but feels more acutely the dangers in that potency. The trope of oxymoron implies recognition of the double-edged, self-betraying capacities of language, the hazard of one's words deluding rather than liberating, for example. The language of enchantment can become a silencing enthrallment. This is the pradoxical crux of Keats's fantasizing, how, as he says at the opening of "The Fall of Hyperion," one may "with a fine spell of words . . . save/Imagination" from "dumb enchantment." (9–11)

Awareness of the power of language to turn against its user renders heroic the poet's commitment in the "Ode to Psyche" and may have been part of the attraction to Keats of *The Golden Ass*, which teaches the danger of curiosity, above all, curiosity about the powers of magic. Lucius' foolish insistence on learning the secrets of witchcraft leads to his transformation into an ass. And the last of Psyche's trials is to bring from Tartarus a closed box containing the "Imprisoned Treasure of Divine Beauty." Her curiosity leads her to open the box, which releases no "Recipe of Beauty" but the "Sleep of Innermost Darkness," which overcomes her until Cupid reawakens her (141). This would seem no inapt parable for the beauty-worshipping poet curious as to the darkest potencies of language, who in weaving his fine spell of words can all too easily become self-enthralled, paying Merlin's "monstrous debt" of being victimized by the potency of a magic his utterance has called forth.

DIVINE REDEMPTION VS. MIRACLES OF SKEPTICISM

However much or little Keats owes directly to *The Golden Ass*, it is useful to observe that the Roman author confronted a situation somewhat analogous to the Romantic poet's. Apuleius' rhetorical artifices, even of the most extreme kind, are to a significant degree functional. Less self-conscious and obstrusively artifical language would be inadequate for effective representation of the strangeness of what passes for normal existence, a life become so bizarre that through simple report it can no longer be described "realistically." Yet, finally, his author-protagonist does transcend both brutal daily realities and black magic by which he has been so asininely victimized. Salvation comes through faith in Isis, in supernaturalism transcending all aspects of the natural world and all resources of language. The most fantastic artifices of rhetoric drop away, as does his asinine form, in the romance's last chapter when Lucius undergoes a true religious experience of conversion. When he becomes a priest of Isis, he shaves his head to symbolize his abandoning of the entangled sensualism of natural life wherein there can be only victimizing natural magic, not transcendental purity. Because through Lucius's story Apuleius can put behind him natural existence, his romance, despite its horrifying elements, is more comic than agonizing. Chilling insight into the exploitation of slave labor (chapter 8), for example, is trivialized by its context of amusing bawdry, and the profoundest testing of language is avoided in favor of relatively superficial rhetorical games, because in the light of the truth of Isis the horror of what humans do to each other fades to insignificance.

For Keats, there is no extralinguistic and supernatural mode of salvation. There is no Keatsian equivalent for Isis, no divinity other than what he can recreate through language by his own imagining. Divine blessing is bestowed on Lucius, but Keats must be self-enchanted. His times and his own enlightened intelligence condemn him to creating for himself whatever magic he may experience and succeed in evoking in his readers. We are, indeed, far from the "happy pieties" sustaining the "*fond*, believing lyre" of superstition. Keats's imagination must be far more personally intense and more self-analytically psychological than Apuleius'. And the involuted artifice of his seemingly simple style must surpass the coarser rhetorical ingenuities of the Roman, whose art, after all, does not attain to poetry.

Keats's Psyche is only his mind. The release in him of the power to project her into his environment does not diminish the critical intelligence with which he confronts that environment. However intensely Keats, to use oddly appropriate modern slang, psyched himself up, he does not claim to have discovered a power beyond his own creative power. There is no transcendence in the "Ode to Psyche." The fulfillment celebrated in the final lines is just as dependent on the poet's imagination as is the opening vision. Keats's achievement here of the power at once to believe and be skeptical is proved by the immediately following greater odes. For each of these centers on a tension between an experience of the potency of creative imagination and enhanced awareness through that experience itself of the resistance to shaping imagination of an already created artifact, the Grecian Urn, of the continuous transformativeness of emotions, Melancholy, or, with the Nightingale, of the eternal evanescing of natural phenomena. The "Ode to a Nightingale," indeed, ends where the "Ode to Psyche" begins: "Do I wake or sleep?"

Keats's most remarkable accomplishment in these odes is surely this conjoining of imaginative freedom with a realization of the restraints the worlds of nature and culture impose upon the powers of fantasizing. Only through a truly liberated exercise of imagination can its effective limits be discerned, while only by its challenge to accepted limits of reality can the fullness of its power be manifested. Such an act requires making use of what Siebers calls "the logic of superstition," substituting for a "fond, believing lyre" one attuned by awareness of the inadequacy of superstitious belief yet willing to explore the potentialities of its forms for confronting a world that defines itself through the exclusion of anything marvelous. This implies recognizing the psychological implications of Tolkien's assertion that the "marvels" of fantasy cannot tolerate "machinery suggesting that the whole story in which they occur is . . . illusion." The principal mechanism for thus explaining away the supernatural—against which explanations fantasy sets itself—is, as Manlove observes, to treat a "marvel" simply "as a disguised projection of something within our 'nature.' "[10] The "Ode to Psyche" is shaped to assure that Psyche will not be such a "disguised projection," but, rather, recognized to be a deliberate recreation by the poet. This recognition explains why the poem's fundamental organizing figure must be oxymoron, a trope, as Rosemary Jackson has rightly asserted, subversive of logical rhetoric, though she fails to trace out in detail how oxymoron supersedes other figures in the mode of fantasy. Only T. E. Apter, so far as I know, has addressed this issue. He points out that fantasy's language not only "defies the systematic representions of allegory," but even passes beyond metaphor by carrying out a "conflation of tenor and vehicle, so that there is "no means of finding the way back to original terms"; in fantasy, "figurative language becomes the only means of making literal assertions."[11]

It is the development of such tropes surpassing tropes that makes Keats's later poems more spiritually powerful, emotionally complex, and intellectually daring than his earlier works, just as the later poetry does not merely regret, nor merely aspire longingly to, the wonder of fantastic experience. In the last poems the full possibilities of fantasizing are provocatively realized because their impossibility is accepted as the condition for their imaginative realization.

How Keats advances from his achievement of self-inspiration in the Psyche ode may briefly be illustrated by the fragmentary *Fall of Hyperion*, which reworks the earlier reworking in *Hyperion* of another neglected episode from classical mythological tradition, the overthrow of the Titans by the Olympians. The central feature of Keats's revision of his earlier poem is his transformation of direct narrative into a dreamvision, the nature and significance of which is represented as problematic. *The Fall of Hyperion*, though about gods, is not from god. Keats's dream-vision is only self-validating. It is worthy of presentation not for its transcendent source but for a possible, though not certain, success at realizing for its readers its translation of Keats's private vision into a verbal artifact worthy of our wonder.

Within the dream, furthermore, both the poet's capability and the worthwhileness of his vision are challenged, and such challenging of vision by vision is an inevitable consequence of "singing by my own eyes inspired." Self-inspired visions' authority can derive only from the *effect* of their representations, which the poet cannot predict with assurance. So exactly what Keats does not strive to become is a traditional, divinely inspired seer or prophet. His visionary poem remains a fantastic one; there is no extrinsic assurance of its cogency or value, as, by implication, there was for *Hyperion* through its direct narration, which at the least predicates for its subject an objective coherence and a temporal significance, both brought into question by *The Fall*, in which myth is remodeled into fantasy. Skepticism inheres within the Keatsian visionary experience, for the dreamer cannot know how valid his dream of dreaming may be, because its validity can only be established by his readers' valuation of his rehearsal of it:

> Whether the dream now purpos'd to rehearse
> Be poet's or fanatic's will be known
> When this warm scribe, my hand, is in the grave.
>   (16–18)

If we accept Foucault's view that any discourse is not merely an intersection of words and things but a practice that constitutes that of which it speaks, that discourse does more than merely use signs to designate things, the primary characteristic of poetry built upon oxymoron must be the uncertainty of its effects, for it seeks to empower our imagination beyond what we have imagined to be its capabilities. This generating of potency out of imagination's self-testing determines even the deployment of individual words, because oxymoron brings to the surface their self-transformative potential, the kind of superabundance of meaning I have pointed to, for example, in the word *vision*. But as important and more visible are analogous thematic affects.

In *The Fall of Hyperion* Keats not only reenvisions his earlier imagining as a dream, but in returning to this subject appears bent on pushing farther into the self-dissolution of the story that has contributed, however marginally, to the Western cultural tradition. The subject, after all, is the rise to power of the Greek pantheon, later to be overthrown by Christianity. Yet Keats's focus is not on the newly triumphant god, as is Milton's in his "Ode on Christ's Nativity," but on the defeated Titan. The title of Keats's revision seems definitive in centering attention on what is lost in the emergence of new divinity, a new object of superstitous belief. His poetry describes where imagination had been but can no longer be. His subject is a cenotaph, an empty tomb, his poetry is sculpture "builded up upon the grave" of its "own power." Yet Keats does not, like some of his successors in the fantastic mode, fall into mere regretful nostalgia, even though,

> nor could my eyes
> And ears act with that pleasant unison of sense
> Which marries sweet sound with the grace of form,
> And dolorous accent from a tragic harp
> With large-limb'd visions. (I, 441–45)

With the success of the Olympian Apollo, Hyperion's fall can be realized only through fantasy, as the disappearance of any genuine superstition means that its recovery must be a self-consciously imagined one. So *The Fall of Hyperion* does for the form of the dream-vision what "La Belle Dame" and "The Ancient Mariner" do for the ballad form: make use of it to articulate what the original form had not in itself fully realized. Keats's intensification of his chosen form is discernible in his making his poem about a dream of dreaming about a dream. He begins, "Methought I stood where trees of every clime," and in that deserted arbor of his thought he drinks a "transparent juice," a "full draught" that is "parent of my theme," plunging him into a swoon. He awakes from this swoon within his dream not in the arbor but a "sanctuary" where he encounters Moneta who there endows him with "a power to see as a God sees" (303), answering his plea, "Let me behold, according as thou saidst" (289), by transporting him in vision "Deep in the shady sadness of a vale" (294), whereupon there grows "A power within me of enormous ken," to "take the depth/Of things as nimbly as the outward eye/Can size and shape pervade" (302–05). Here he must bear "The load of this eternal quietude" (390), and "Oftentimes I pray'd/Intense, that death would take me from the vale/And all its burthens" (396–98). And the poet's doubt at the end of the first canto that he may "perhaps no further dare" (468) in this recursive envisioning applies to the reader, for only those "may read who can unwearied pass/Onward from the antechamber of this dream" (464–65).

The necessity for this recessive sequence, which provides a model for how the Romantics believe we should approach all imaginative literature of the past, by reimagining ourselves into its lost source of energy, appears most plainly in the difference between Keats's mode of reading his dreams and Freud's procedure. Freud interprets dreams by giving a rational explanation of them. A Freudian interpretation translates the fantastic discourse of dream into the discourse of critical rationality so as to make the meaningless intelligible by displaying what is latent within its absurd manifest surface. By dreaming of a dream of dreaming Keats interprets in an entirely different fashion. Exactly what he refuses to do is to translate the fantastic into the rational. Instead, he inscribes his skeptical critical intelligence into his fantastic dreaming. That is why both the experience and his reporting of it must be so intensely painful and why the result, the interpretation that is the story of his recursive dream, must be so problematic, with no decisive Freudian explanation, but the dramatization of a possibility for the reader imaginatively to explore. What we see in the last part of the *Fall of Hyperion* is the narrator struggling (and because the poem is incomplete, failing) both to endure and understand the meaning of the supernatural vision offered him by Moneta. Freud is committed to the position that any fantasy, ideally at least, is interpretable in the sense of being at root rationally explicable by being translated into the terms of conventional scientific language. The doubtfulness of the imaginative experience of Hyperion's fall as represented by Keats is not guaranteed by him to be so meaningful; it cannot be explained as Freud explains, for it is accessible only to inspired perception that can accept it as not belonging to reality defined by the terms of normal, rationalized, scientific discourse.[12]

In this respect *The Fall* pushes farther the opening question of the "Ode to Psyche," helping us to understand that the relation between seeing with awakened or dreaming eyes is best not reduced to simple antithesis. It is better to enlarge the relation by pursuing all possible meanings and implications of dreaming. This pursuit, however, cannot be carried on by wakeful reason alone, but requires us to dream about dreaming. This process (and perhaps this process alone) gives us uncondescending access to superstitions that have been exploded, and therefore are not available to incredulous rationality, without, however, requiring us to abandon reason. To the contrary, if we can bear the strain, reason can be inscribed within a discourse enriched in tacit dimensions, marvelous because both circumscribed and penetrated by the unknown, the undefined, the not yet experienced.

Keats presents the reader of his late works with opportunities to go beyond accepted limits of what is imaginable in complete awareness of the conventional baselessness of allowing one's mind such freedom. The Psyche ode is important in Keats's career because once the poet gains the confidence to sing "by my own eyes inspired" he is liberated from both the symmetrical tyrannies of naive superstitousness and unexamined faith in sheer rationality. At this moment all the exciting self-conflicts of the late poetry become feasible. But Keats's accomplishments were cut short by his tragically early death, and they were neither consolidated nor pushed farther by his Victorian and Modern successors.

DECLINE INTO POETIC PROSE

That Romantic fantasy did not prosper after Keats's death is indisputable. Most subsequent fantasists in the nineteenth and twentieth centuries are relatively minor figures who favored prose over poetry, though often affecting poetic prose. Representatively illustrative is Lord Dunsany, whose style dramatizes even in its successes a characteristic falling away from Keatsian

intensity. Dunsany's work is especially interesting because virtually all of his fantasy is a lamentation for the loss of the power to
fantasize.

Dunsany writes with wit and elegance, but, because he does
not believe in his own fantasizing, as Keats was able to believe
in Psyche and La Belle Dame, Dunsany attains charm rather
than profundity. *The Charwoman's Shadow*, his best novel,
though superior to the better known works of Chamisso and
Hoffmansthal which utilize the motif of the lost shadow, remains
a lovely minor work because it confines itself to describing the
loss of magic from our world. Significantly, the protagonist
Ramon Alonzo never masters the art of magic; the one love
potion he concocts very nearly kills the prince who drinks it. And
the spectacular final pages of the novel depict the defeated
magician carrying all magic out of the novel's vivid evocations of
Spanish landscapes and lives of "ordinary fields" and "ordinary
tears." Dunsany's skill lies in arousing nostalgia for fantasy rather
than creating fantasy; unlike Keats, he never enchants himself,
so he can cast but a superficial spell on his readers.

This weakness appears even in what many consider Dunsany's finest short story, "The Sword of Welleran," in which the
incantatory style is marvelously appropriate to his poignant plot,
which concerns the saving of the city of Merimna. The city once
had powerful armies that scourged its enemies under the leader-
ship successively of "Welleran, Soorenard, Mommolek, Rollory,
Akanax, and young Iraine."[13] These warrior-leaders who built up
the luxurious and art-filled city are believed by Merimna's
enemies not to have died but magically remain to defend the city
against attack. Eventually, however, enemies learn that the
figures of the leaders they see on the ramparts are but statues
wondrously carved, and armies come in the night to surprise the
city. But the souls of the dead leaders drift from paradise to the
sleeping city and enter the dreams of the citizens, who arise and
take up their arms. Welleran enters the dreams of a boy named
Rold, "as a butterfly flits through trellis-work into a garden of
flowers," and inspires him to go to the center of Merimna and
take from its case the cloak and famous sword of Welleran, with
which he leads the defense against the night attack.

And the savage, lusting sword that had thirsted for a
hundred years went up with the hand of Rold and swept
through a tribesman's ribs. And with the warm blood all
about it there came a joy into the curved soul of that
mighty sword. . . . [And] when they saw the red cloak
and that terrible sword a cry ran through the tribal
armies, "Welleran lives!" And there arose the sounds of
the exulting of victorious men, and the panting of those
that fled, and the sword singing softly to itself as it
whirled dripping through the air . . . falling, gleaming
blue in the moonlight whenever it arose and afterwards
gleaming red, and so disappearing into the darkness.
(114–15)

With the dawn Rold sees the victory that the sword of
Welleran has wrought.

"O sword, sword! How horrible thou art! . . . How
many eyes shall look upon gardens no more because of
thee? How many fields must go empty that might have
been fair with cottages, white cottages, with children all
about them? . . . I hear the wind crying against thee,
thou sword! It comes from the empty valleys. It comes
from the bare fields. There are children's voices in it.
They were never born. . . ." And the tears of Rold fell
down upon the proud sword but could not wash it clean.
(115)

And Rold's enlightened sorrow is echoed by the citizens, for
whom this victory brings to an end their faith in their magic
inviolability: "Not any more, not any more for ever will Welleran
now return, for his sword is in the hand of another. Now
we know indeed that he is dead" (115). The power of this
ironic conclusion, one observes, lies in the disappearance from
Merimna of magic. So it is appropriate that the incantatory style
of the story turns away from adventuresome revelations of
complex potencies and intricate self-testings undergirding the
recursive structuring of Keats's maturest poetry—as well as the
very different but equally dense style of his fellow Romantic,
Heinrich von Kleist, and even that of a major postmodern reviver
of Romantic fantasy, Gabriel García Márquez.

CHAPTER SEVEN

Romantic Fantasy and Postmodern Fiction

The brutal existential shock of occasionally discovering we live
in a world of strange objects and events that totally escape our
system of perception is a reminder of the precariousness of our
fictional reality.

LUIS HARSS, "Macondo, Huevo Filosofico"

Liker Death than He

SAMUEL COLERIDGE,
"The Rime of the Ancient Mariner" (1798)

UNSANY'S POETIC PROSE GIVES INSIGHT INTO ONE
central problem besetting fantasy in prosaic
narrative form after the Romantic era. Because faith had been lost in the value of
fantasy, most writers attempting it felt a need
to dress it up, and Sir Walter Scott seemed to
provide them with the ideal costume. The
success of Scott's historical romances was a fatally seductive
model for fictional reconstructions of societies in which belief in
the supernatural and magic had existed. Through a retreat into
the past, one could portray superstition realistically. This may
seem to be what Coleridge does in "The Ancient Mariner," but in
fact, by concentrating his artistry on creation of the falsely
archaic form of the ballad, Coleridge skillfully avoids justifying
the supernatural events in the poem as merely historically valid.
His poem, like all the best Romantic fantasy, is shaped so as to
impress its reader as dealing not with what might have happened,
or with what some people might have thought could happen, but
with what, however surprising and improbable, did actually
occur. Contrarily, historical fiction containing elements of fantasy, novels about societies without novels, usually functioned to
subvert the creation of genuine fantasy, and, indeed, provided a
basis for the development of the modern concept of the primitive
which was to become a favored device for doing away with the

117

fantastic. And by the paternalistic association of the primitive with the immature, which Freud so brilliantly systematized, fantasy was defined as a genre of children's literature.

To become something more than a minor, belletristic accomplishment, to appeal to adults as well as children, fantasy in our century has had to devise new aesthetic strategies. Fantasists have had to seek what the science fiction writer avoids, innovations in narrative modes. Science fiction writers do not wish to bring into question accepted systems of determining and describing the possible, for their art is dependent on extrapolation from what is accepted as possible. They must establish a sense of probability. But for a fantasist, who desires to realize the oxymoron of the possible-impossible, bringing into question all forms of naturalistic narrative and description must be a preeminent ambition. So the historically sophisticated fantasist treating the past will find a way to misuse traditional forms deriving from earlier times. Thus Keats and Coleridge misuse the ballad, as Henry James superbly misuses the fairy tale in *The Turn of the Screw*. These successful fantasists turn traditional forms against themselves, making the forms do what they had not traditionally done. Keats and Coleridge, as I have suggested, carry the ballad beyond itself in a Shakespearian manner, and illustrative of an analogous creative subversion of prosaic forms are the tales of E. T. A. Hoffmann. Even more revealing, because more directly forcing its reader to confront the significance of possibilities of distortion in realistic historical narrative, is Heinrich von Kleist's *Michael Kohlhaas*, which brilliantly misuses what it cites as its authorizing source in its subtitle, an *Old Chronicle*.

JUSTICE AS REVENGE

The fine translators of the Penguin edition of *Michael Kohlhaas* in their introduction fault the novella for gratuitously introducing an element of fantasy.

> Kleist . . . introduced a bizarre and fantastic sub-plot which seriously damages the artistic structure of an already long and complex narrative . . . Kleist was

certainly motivated by an artistically extraneous desire
to discredit Saxony . . . His reasons for adding the
gypsy episode may also have included a literary inten-
tion, misguided in this case, of deliberately creating
mystery.[1]

But in fact *Michael Kohlhaas* is a powerful work of art because
the logic of its realism is so functionally complicated by the
intrusion of bizarre supernaturalism. Whatever Kleist's antipathy
to Saxony, it was his genius that led him to distort the rationalistic naturalism that is the limit of his translators' admiration. The
novella's shattering effect results from its displaying both the
representational and ethical inadequacy of realistic narrative—
an effect disturbing, one may note, to many of Kleist's contemporaries, including Goethe.

The truly vexing problem in *Michael Kohlhaas* is the relation
or nonrelation of its supernaturalism to Christianity, a problem
as I have already noted that haunts criticism of "The Ancient
Mariner." In Kleist's story one several times must wonder if
Christianity is not being satirized. In the prison scene, for
example, the old woman chosen to impersonate the gypsy not
only turns out to be the gypsy, but also seems to be Kohlhaas's
pious wife Elisabeth, killed early in the tale. A similar conjoining
of chance and ambigous spirituality, along with humor, charac-
terizes several episodes. Kohlhaas, about to burn down the
nunnery in which he thinks the Junker hides (a moment made
ludicrous by the overage porter struggling to get his armor on),
changes his mind abruptly, apparently because a lightning bolt
strikes close to him and the abbess. But the reader cannot be sure
that Kohlhaas takes the bolt as a warning, nor would it be
unreasonable to think, if the bolt does come from God, that it
was intended as a rebuke to the abbess.

The profoundest spiritual ambiguity is focused by the representation of Martin Luther. The very strength of Kohlhaas's
simple faith in Luther causes one to find causuistical several of
Luther's arguments. And, as the divine himself is forced to
recognize, at times his condemnation seems less cogent than

Kohlhaas' defense of his actions. Even Luther's claim that the Brandenburg Elector is innocent because ignorant, a "good" ruler, just not informed by his subordinates of what was happening, is too ingenious not to raise doubts about Luther's motives. The practical effect of accepting Luther's proposals for Kohlhaas is to put himself in a position to be dishonorably betrayed and imprisoned in Dresden. Yet, perhaps because both Luther's judgment and intentions are in their very articulation made suspect, his urging of Kohlhaas to forgive his enemy must impress us as morally forceful: this seems a clear and honest appeal to the essential spirit of Christianity. By resisting Luther's demand and clinging to his desire for retribution, Kohlhaas appears to compromise his religious convictions. Still, the arrogance of Luther's manner of insisting that Kohlhaas forgive, as well as his arrogation to himself of the right to judge for Christ, tends to make us sympathize with Kohlhaas's tenacity of purpose, perhaps even to wonder what Luther himself knows of charity. And charity, that central Christian virtue, poses a question to justice which the novella in diverse fashions reiterates with painful acuity.

Because the story's action centers on Kohlhaas's simultaneous search for and destruction of justice, it must carry us beyond its own vivid dramatizing of the conflict between bourgeois commercialism and bureaucratic feudalism, even though that competition between social classes is consistently foregrounded. Just as Kohlhaas readily affirms that one of his motives in seeking justice is his need for conditions in which he can successfuly carry on his business, so the Saxon aristocracy makes small pretense among themselves that their persecution of him is righteous rather than self-interested. The openness with which these unheroic motives are exhibited lays the groundwork for evocation of our ambivalent feelings when Kohlhaas cheerfully concurs in having his head struck off after the Junker has been compelled to fatten this horses. In the grandly formalized final scene, rendered like a painting by Veronese, one is forced to recognize how hideously absurd becomes the working out in practice of a reasonable justice, a recognition that must make painfully problematic any belief in the intrinsic goodness of enlightened society.

The pain is fierce because of the emotional force Kleist generates by his representations of injustice. Every reader shares Kohlhaas's outrage at the unfair persecution he undergoes. Every reader is compelled to participate in the protagonists's loathing of the junker and the despicable system of bureaucracy that sustains him. So powerfully are our feelings aroused and so precisely directed that we gloatingly share Kohlhaas's satisfaction in the last scene when in front of the Saxon Elector he reads the prophetic message and then swallows the paper on which it is written. But our enjoyment must be tempered by Kohlhaas's genial acceptance of his beheading, for this constitutes admission that his behavior has been monstrous—as, indeed, it has. Do we take satisfaction in behaving monstrously? We finish the novella with strongly conflicted feelings. From these we may learn our need to resist the compulsions such emotions enforce. The satisfaction we share with Kohlhaas in his revenge we must learn to condemn, for that satisfaction is monstrous. It is monstrous because it makes us a victim of emotion, not its master, and thereby perverts our outrage at injustice into new injustice.

The grim joy of vengeance, whose root meaning is the same as vindication, is represented as darkness visible by Kohlhaas' feelings just before his wife dies. "In the midst of his grief at seeing the world in such monstrous disorder, an inward sense of contentment now flooded over him" (MK, 131) when he realizes that the Junker will not forestall his revenge by returning his horses. The blasphemous savagery of this so comforting feeling is reinforced by the scene of Elizabeth's death (MK, 137).

> Then she turned to Kohlhaas, who was sitting on her bed, and pointed with her finger at the verse: "Forgive your enemies; do good also unto them that hate you"; whereupon, pressing his hand, she gazed at him with deep emotion and expired. Kohlhaas thought to himself: "May God never forgive me as I forgive the Junker!"

The true meaning of this threat we understand when we see Kohlhaas's groom Hesse, who had restrained himself from blowing up the Junker's castle because he heard a child cry out within it, following Kohlhaas's orders and throwing out of the castle window the bodies of women and children he has murdered. Revenge dehumanizes, but its emotional satisfaction is so delicious that few, especially those vigorous in their feelings of virtuousness, and those outraged by injustice, can resist it. *Michael Kohlhaas* teaches the terrible truth that there can be profound joy in dehumanizing oneself.

Aeschylus directly represented such feelings in the *Oresteia*, but in the early nineteenth century Kleist faced the trickier task of dramatizing more complex displacements and concealments of the sinister delights Aeschylus had revealed. All modern states claim that their system of legal justice eliminates entirely personal revenge. But modern legal justice, Kleist would force us to recognize, only disguises the emotional systematics of retributive vengeance. The primary means of so disguising is through the most fundamental vehicle for juridical organization: writing. This is why to the title of the novella is affixed the information, *From an Old Chronicle*, although the inadequacies of this source are lamented throughout the account. The action of the narrative begins with a demand for a written permit and concludes with the swallowing of a paper on which is written a supernaturally informed prediction. Everywhere in the story from casual details to pivotal plot developments—Luther uncomfortably pushing papers about on his desk when troubled by Kohlhaas' sincerity, the true-false letter of Nagelschmidt that allows the Dresden authorities to arrest the horse dealer—writing appears in a fashion suggesting its inherently deceitful or misleading qualities. Writing is persistently associated with the exercise of unjust power and arbitrary violence. Although this association poses problems of interpretation, it more significantly raises the issue of writing's intrinsic distortion of actuality simply by being writing. In *Michael Kohlhaas*, the written document, the foundation of all legal authority in civilized societies, appears as inherently a falsification, necessarily reducing the complex contingencies of experience to an arbitrary order empowering one person or one group at the expense of others. Kohlhaas is victimized by legal documents fabricated by the von Tronkas. By means of his printed proclamations he asserts, and obtains through thus attracting followers into his insurrectionary army, a power which forces the Saxon authorities to yield to him.

Repeatedly it is made plain that what renders writing dangerous is its narrowing, diminishing, and simplifying of realities to which it pretends to refer comprehensively. Writing consistently implies or demands comprehensibility, but all language, especially in its nonostensive, written form, must arbitrarily impose limited and limiting structures on a world fecund in contingencies. Because isolated from the circumstances of oral communication, language in its written form most disastrously violates the intricacy of phenomenal existence.

Writing in its fixity and absoluteness fails to do justice to the uncertainties, the randomness, and chance elements that play so large a part in human affairs as they are represented in *Michael Kohlhaas*, most spectacularly perhaps in the Breughelesque scene in the Dresden marketplace when the confrontation between the chamberlain and the knacker leads to a general riot. But the novella also links writing to the compulsiveness of emotionality that also limits, narrows, and reduces the fullest and freest potentialities of the human spirit. Thus by encouraging us to share the feelings driving Kohlhaas to revenge, the very writing that constitutes the novella tempts us into experiencing the sweet self-poisoning pleasure of revenge. Because we are so caught up by these written words, we can appreciate (if we exercise a self-consciously critical scrutiny of our sentiments) how feeble an opponent to outraged feeling is mere rationality. We come to understand through our experience of *Michael Kohlhaas* that what passes for reason is likely to be emotion attentuated, disguised, displaced. We recognize, therefore, that reason, like emotion, though less directly, is a function of a system of reciprocities, that reason works because contained within a closed structure. *Michael Kohlhaas* is a fearful fiction, for it forces us feel how both reason and emotion confine us within closed patterns of arbitrary determinism whose product is violence.

Any legal system is an arbitrary patterning of impulses, a systematized displacing of passions from which the legal system in fact derives its force. But the indirection intrinsic to legality assures that more often than not, either through accident or deliberate manipulation, it will frustrate the emotions it seeks to channel. Pure, straightforward vengeance satisfies because it allows for no interference with nor redirection of fulfillment of outraged feelings. It does indeed release an inward flood of contentment.

It would be a serious misreading of *Michael Kohlhaas* to claim that the novella criticizes vengeance because it is archaic or because it is irrational. Kleist's work strives to make us realize that vengeance, though disguised, functions today as vigorously as ever, even though we teach ourselves to believe we have replaced it by concepts of logical legality. And what is wrong with revenge is that in either its ancient, direct form, or in its modern concealed form, the impulse to vengeance imprisons the individual who enjoys it within an inescapable compulsion of reciprocal violences. Vengeance denies the possibility of breaking free of the mode of existence defined by its operation. In accepting vengeance in any form we bind ourselves to behavior that is deterministic, totally unfree, destructive of our best human capabilities.

This is why Kleist's novella can be perceived as attacking not merely the legalistic rationalism of Enlightenment thinking, for which Rousseau's *Social Contract* can be taken as representative, but also those who, like Edmund Burke, celebrated the beneficent effects of traditional patterns of behavior. *Michael Kohlhaas* suggests that escape from compulsive violence lies only in a radical revalorizing of forgiveness. Both intellectually and emotionally forgiveness is an asystematic act. Especially within the dubiously Christian ambiance of the novella, the act of forgiveness appears as wildly unreasonable. But it is made equally plain that forgiving an injury reverses a natural system of emotive responses. This is why to forgive is the most liberative action of which human beings are capable. Forgiveness is the most humanizing of acts, for by forgiving we break the chain of emotional determinism in which we morally imprison ourselves when we yield to the impulse for vengeance. And society encourages us so to enslave ourselves through its disguising of such impulses as impersonal legal codes.

Forgiveness is urged on Kohlhaas both by his wife and by Martin Luther, but he refuses. By refusing, he remains a man simultaneously honorable and horrible, one whose profound desire for justice necessarily drives him into becoming a murderer and incendiary, because the justice he desires is a reciprocal balance that is ultimately indistinguishable from revenge—as is dramatized masterfully in the final scene. Here the full panoply of legalized justice is displayed as if in an official allegorical painting, "The Wisdom and Righteousness of the Empire." But the formalizations of legality represented are in fact bizarre to the point of insanity. Kohlhaas' delight that Herse's old mother should get back her bundle of laundry, and his readiness to be decapitated are explicable only as a reciprocal of his unholy joy in gaining revenge on the von Tronkas and on the Saxon Elector. And at this point the grounds for the state to insist on the execution of Kohlhaas are his behavior after he had been unfairly declared to be an outlaw. The justice of his extreme punishment, therefore, boils down to no more than the exaction of an eye for an eye.

The forgiveness Kohlhaas rejects is a conscious act, a deliberate choice. It implies—amazingly—that one can break free from, thereby to reshape, the total emotional structure of one's life. Forgiveness is the ultimate act of emotional creativity, for it cannot come into being as a mere unthinking response, since it is by definition a deliberate reversal of the current of one's feeling. But forgiveness is not only a rational act. True forgiveness is not mere suppression or repression of anger or hate but, instead, the transformation of those passions into a bestowal of love.

This Kleistian representation of forgiveness is most significantly Romantic because *Michael Kohlhaas* is not simply an apology for traditional Christian doctrine, which, indeed, the novella represents as problematical at best. Kleist portrays Martin Luther in a fashion that compels us to question his spiritual wisdom, perhaps even his practical motives. Nor is it accidental that the novella is set in the era of the Reformation, the epoch of Christianity's profoundest self-challenge. *Michael Kohlhaas* makes no simple claim to any conventional piety. And the crux of Romantic resistance to Enlightenment systematizing lies in the absence from it of any direct or conventionally approved appeal to some justifying suprarational power. The Romantics deploy fantastic elements, invoke supernaturalism, to criticize rational systematizing from a position of transcendental groundlessness. The fantastic, in short, is a Romantic mode for effecting a skeptical critique of skeptical thought itself. So the fantastic or supernatural elements in *Michael Kohlhaas*, however peripheral they may seem to modern translators, are essential. Only an inexplicable and totally unconventional supernaturalism makes possible a testing not of one kind of authority but of the very concept of authority itself, which is one of the central functions of *Michael Kohlhaas*—and much of the best Romantic literature.

Readers of Kleist's novella understand why Kohlhaas is driven to identify himself with the archangel Michael, but regard him as misguided. Readers understand why the elector believes in the gypsy's prophetic powers, but do not share his persuasion. As the novella thus increases a reader's skepticism about what the characters so passionately believe, it becomes difficult for readers to see any order but what is arbitrarily (and hence erroneously) imposed on circumstances portrayed realistically, that is to say, with all aspects of contingency and all the confusions of misguided and conflicting purposes foregrounded. Yet to accept the full implications of this perspective will be to perceive the absurdity of claims that there can be rational justice, and to recognize that justice as normally defined is a disguise for sheer power. Indisputably in a universe without inherent order, where chance determines, might is right. And if our world is composed chiefly of arbitrary structures imposed on it by fallible human beings, the impositions of the strongest will prevail. To call such impositions justice would be to mock the very skeptical intelligence enabling us to criticize the various delusions of understanding manifested by the characters in Kleist's story.

This definitional impasse explains why Kleist constructs his narrative to agitate our emotions so violently. It is the outrage we feel against what is done to Kohlhaas that empowers our desire that he be avenged. Kohlhaas himself impresses us favorably because he is so true to his strongest feelings, and so honest about what he feels. Profoundly as he loves his children, whom he carries about and nurses tenderly, he exults more in revenging himself on the elector: the sacrifice of his life is not too high a price for the joy of vengeance. As one considers the conflict of sentiments which the novella arouses at the conclusion, one comes to realize that what Kohlhaas lacks is imagination. Imagination enables one to forgive. Kohlhaas cannot forgive, as his wife and Luther ask him to, because in fact he desires, as we gradually become aware, literal, material justice, an unimaginative justice, not spiritual nor metaphysical justice. Admirable as Kohlhaas is, his mind never moves beyond the physical conditions of his horses, or the bundle of laundry. His literalism creates the complications that eventually involve the entire empire, because what is most difficult to satisfy (indeed, what is impossible to satisfy) is a demand for literal justice. There is nothing with which to buy Kohlhaas off; there are for him no equivalent compensations; only fat on his horses will do, no abstract or symbolic recompense is possible for him.

The sinister side of this materialism that is, to be sure, attractive (Kohlhaas's honesty has charm because rooted in this down-to-earth concreteness) is dramatized when Kohlhaas eats the prophetic paper, for this act gives us appalling insight into the essential vengefulness of a commitment to literal, material justice. Kohlhaas epitomizes the fundamental basis of bourgeois virtues, certainly more attractive than that feeble embodiment of feudalistic corruption, the Saxon Elector. Yet it is Kohlhaas who must, finally, be judged, even by a bourgeois reader, as a terrible man, because he carries to its limit that moral virtue of justice found on the satisfaction of outraged feelings which can only masquerade as legal right.

The admirable Kohlhaas could not function to reveal the monstrosity of moral virtue were it not for the introduction into a naturalistic narrative of elements of fantasy. The gypsy woman's first appearance is not necessarily fantastic, for her prediction about the stag could be explained in realistic terms, although the sequence of contingencies involved (along with the Bradenburg Elector's understandable delight at her prophetic power) allow us to appreciate why the Saxon Elector gives unswerving credence to her supernatural gifts. Nor is it impossible that, without being known to Kohlhaas, she might know of him and his situation. But the gypsy's second appearance is not only incredible but is so described by the text. Her selection as the agent to impersonate herself, as the narrator takes pains to observe, constitutes an improbability so extreme that "who so pleases is at liberty to doubt it" (MK, 206–07). On this occasion, moreover, the old woman begins to bear an uncanny resemblance to Kohlhaas's dead wife, even to a mole on her neck, while the family dog gives every sign of recognizing his former mistress. Her farewell speech to Kohlhaas—"till we meet again, when there won't be anything of these things you won't know" (MK, 208)—referring to his desire to learn how she possesses her knowledge, and why she has chosen to help him, suggests some sort of supernatural reunion, a possibility reinforced by the signature on her final note, "Your Elizabeth." Thus at the conclusion of the tale we are made to feel sure that some more than natural power is at work in events, but this assurance only makes more problematic the relation of material and spiritual forces in the story. Practically, and even ideologically, Kohlhaas's determination to be revenged makes perfectly good sense, so long as we are content with a bourgeois view of reality, and remain untroubled by the idea that what we call justice may merely be vengeance in disguise. Only if we break free of a materialistic view of things, only by coming to question the adequacy to free human beings of a deterministic conception of the world is it possible for us to articulate what is wrong with revenge. For those lacking religious faith, that is to say, virtually all enlightened minds of the past two centuries, fantasy is one of the few means for so liberating us.

Michael Kohlhaas is certainly not a work advocating Christian faith, but it is a work that raises doubts about the effects of skeptical rejections of belief in anything other than natural phenomena and of a materialistic view of the world. The principal system of belief referred to in the story is Christianity. Like "The Rime of the Ancient Mariner, Michael Kohlhaas, is

located in the past not to provide a spurious historical justification for supernatural events but to create a temporalized cultural
perspective permitting a distinction to emerge between the
beliefs of people within the tale and the nonbelief of readers of
the tale. The purpose of the distinction is not to validate earlier
beliefs but to force the latter-day skeptics into self-judgment.
This purpose identifies the novella as Romantic, and Romantic
also is its assumption that the principal antagonist to skeptical
thought is Christianity. However much Kleist's work expresses
the increasing secularization of Western culture, it accepts
Christianity as the dominant form for supernatural belief. This
makes fantasy a serious matter, for it exposes its creator to the
risk of confronting a charge of blasphemy. The Romantic's risk
bestowed on him, however, an advantage over his successors
writing for an increasingly secularized public: the Romantic
could address the problem of supernatural potency as a vital
issue. Both a Voltairean sophisticate and a naive Christian had
reason to be upset by Kleist's unorthodox invocations of supernaturalism.

The history of fantasy later in the nineteenth century and
into our own times is in good measure the history of its
progressive loss of power to disturb in increasingly secularized
societies. The nadir of this diminishment is marked by Freud's
success at demolishing with a scientific psychology all serious
attention to the supernatural, his naturalizing of the supernatural. Yet Kleist's novella and the poetry of Coleridge and Keats
continue to fascinate readers, and as the influence of Modernism
has waned, fantasy has begun to attract the attention of literary
critics. More important, in recent years several major writers of
fiction have begun to reexplore the potentialities of fantasy, and
of these, none more efficaciously than Gabriel García Márquez.
His very brief story "The Last Voyage of the Ghost Ship"
illustrates cogently the nature and direction of this revival, and,
if it does not surely foretell something of the future of the
literature of fantasy, it vividly highlights the peculiar circumstances within which fantasy today can come into being.

To treat García Márquez as a fantasist, however, is to fly in
the face of his adamant and repeated denials that he writes

fantasy. Perhaps his most amusingly defiant statement occurs in a short essay that was translated in *Harper's Magazine* under the title of "Latin America's Impossible Reality."

> Fantasy is that which has nothing to do with the reality of the world we live in; it is a purely fantastic invention, an inspiration, and certainly a diversion ill-advised in the arts . . . no one would argue that fantasy is the creative virtue of Franz Kafka; . . . there is no doubt that it is the genius of Walt Disney. Contrary to what the dictionary says, I believe that imagination is the particular faculty artists possess that enables them to create a new reality from the one they live in. That is the only artistic creation that seems valid to me.[2]

And he goes on to say:

> In the Caribbean to the original elements—primitive myths and magical conceptions—was added a bountiful variety of cultures . . . in the crossroads of the world was forged a sense of freedom without end, a reality with neither god nor law.

Granting that García Márquez uses a Spanish dictionary (*imaginario* and *fantasia* do not have exactly the same connotations as their English equivalents), and that he is never unwilling to tease his critics, I believe the foregoing is an acurate definition of his endeavors in works such as "The Ghost Ship." García Márquez creates a reality that differs from normal reality, that is impossible according to conventional definitions of the real, but that is not for that reason dismissable as unreal. This pushes him into a contemporary mode of the discourse of oxymoron characteristic of Romantic fantasy, a discourse that comes into being because of a writer's refusal to accept the conventional ideas of what is real that his society would enforce upon him. A major difference between his imaginative works such as "The Last Voyage of the Ghost Ship" and, say, "The Rime of the Ancient Mariner," lies in the matrix of García Márquez' creativity being, as he suggests, the multiculturality of his Caribbean setting. The impossible reality of his fiction derives less from a self-conscious exploitation of earlier ways of thinking, and belief in the creation of an enhanced version of a traditional form, such as the ballad, embodying those ways of thinking and believing, than from a deliberate construction of a newly fluid narrative structure for representing the improbability of contemporary actualities resulting from sociocultural interpenetrations. This structure accommodates the confluence of diverse convictions and traditions. These, having lost their potency as individualized features of a national literature or as expressive of specific social or racial communities, are merged into a new literary form whose originality embodies the weirdness of the intermixing of socially or culturally groundless discourses.

One must understand García Márquez's disclaimers in the light of details like that of the chair which kills the mother of the protagonist in "The Ghost Ship." Dating from "the days of Francis Drake," bought at auction in a "Turk's store," the chair comes to be regarded as "murderous" and is destroyed by the villagers (who ostracize the orphaned son because it was his mother who brought this "throne of misfortune" into the village). The villagers fear the chair because the mother and four other women die after sitting in it, for "it had been used so much over the centuries that its power for giving rest had been used up."[3] García Márquez's phrasing leaves us uncertain whether the explanation of the chair's murderousness is his, or the villagers', or both, but even a reader who interprets the explanation as a village superstition is forced by García Márquez' language to reconsider his view of chairs and their functions. Is it possible that a chair's power of giving rest can be used up? How one answers such a bizarre question matters less than the fact that we have been compelled to think about chairs in a new and unconventional way. The arrangement of words, one might say, creates a new reality of chair possibilities. This is essentially equivalent to the effects of the fantasy I have heretofore discussed: the story demands that we accept as fact (however we interpret the circumstance) that five women sat in a chair brocaded "from the casket of a queen," felt their blood turn "to chocolate," and died. Unless we insist on explaining the phenomenon away by asserting that it was just a funny series of coincidences, or that the teller is insane or pulling our leg, we must confront the possibility of a phenomenal reality operating according to systems other than those to which we have habituated ourselves. One difference between García Márquez's fantasy and that of the Romantics is that he works without benefit of any tradition of otherness, from within a world so totally humanized that even the possibility of supernaturalism has been forgotten. The most visible evidences of this difference are the Romantics' use of Christian frames of reference and their exploitation of archaic forms such as ballad or chronicle which are no longer available to García Márquez, who must therefore invent new structures of discourse,

That is why, stylistically, he is more extreme, although the notorious dense complexity of Kleist's prose accurately foreshadows this later art. Although Kleist exploits the tendency of "old chronicles" to be abrupt in their transitions and not to follow our conceptions of systematic logical progression, like Coleridge writing "The Ancient Mariner" more balladically than any true ballad, Kleist infinitely enriches the knotted density of meaning produced by the awkward syntax of some chronicles. His sentences are often long and contorted not because they are clumsily composed but rather because they are so crammed with ideas, sensations, evaluations, and perspectives so diverse and incommensurate that the sentence can only just contain them, even as the plots of the stories are just barely able to make coherent the superabundance of events they encompass. Although passages such as the long second paragraph of *Michael Kohlhaas* have been analyzed as spectacular illustrations of Kleist's simultaneous complexification of syntax and story,[4] for the sake of brevity I'll cite here the relatively brief first sentence of another of Kleist's stories, "The Earthquake in Chile." "In Santiago, the capital of the kingdom of Chile, at the moment of the great earthquake of 1647 in which many thousands lost their lives, a young Spaniard called Jeronimo Rugera was standing beside one of the pillars in the prison to which he had been commited on a criminal charge, and was about to hang himself" (MK, 51). The compaction of style here reflects what might be called the narrative oxymoron that is the foundation of the plot, the suicide saved at the very instant of self-execution by a natural catastrophe killing thousands and freeing him by destroying the prison in which he was incarcerated for begetting a child on a woman he devoutly loves. The completion of the narrative, echoing the structure of the opening sentence, is the killing in a church of the reunited lovers by priest-inspired mob, their child being saved when the mob mistakenly smashes out the brains of the child of the lovers' best friend. García Márquez' style in "The Ghost Ship" can be regarded as a development of tendencies becoming visible in Kleist's extraordinary prose and responsive to an increased attentuation of specific literary sources. "The Ghost Ship" is constituted of a single sentence, the logical end point of Kleist's elaborative syntax, encompassing not the contradictions and antinomies of a univocal historical tradition but the flowing together of a variety of diverse cultural and literary elements, which, having lost rootedness in their indigenous contexts, are made to float freely into a new and newly unstable unity, the unity of the fantastic story, of García Márquez' imagined reality.

I have stressed the throne of misfortune in "The Ghost Ship" both because it is a pivot of the plot—the unjust ostracism of the protagonist because of his mother's purchase produces his determination to be revenged on the villagers—and because the throne of misfortune in miniature reproduces the effect of the story as a whole. At its conclusion the ghost ship actually smashes aground in the village, leaving the reader to contemplate, along with the dumbfounded villagers, what is impossible but now indisputably exists. A critical alternative might seem to be to describe the whole story as a delusion of the protagonist. But to deny the actuality of the "largest ocean liner in this world and the other" with "the ancient and languid waters of the seas of death dripping down its sides" is simply to refuse to experience the story, to refuse to entertain the possibility of otherness it offers to share with us, its readers. The alternative is, in fact, a way not of interpreting the story but of dismissing it.

Like *Michael Kohlhaas*, "The Ghost Ship" is a tale of revenge. " 'Now they're going to see who I am,' he said to himself," the story begins. And as the "cataclysm" of the "fearsome liner" slams ashore in front of the village church, this

adolescent becoming adult shouts, " 'there it is, you cowards.' "
But García Márquez has none of Kleist's characteristically Romantic interest in justice. The Romantic provides no moral or
religious solution to the problem he dramatizes, but that problem
concerns the basis for moral authority. García Márquez' focus on
the confluence of different times and cultures commits him to a
primary concern simply with bearing witness: "there it is, you
cowards." Only by implication can he raise questions of moral
judgment, for his achievement is creating means for describing a
flowing together of a multitude of ways of thinking, perceiving,
judging, behaving. In the essay cited above, as elsewhere, he
proclaims the Caribbean as a fecund junction point of myths,
magics, and cultures, a uniquely rich "crossroads of the world."
Into "The Ghost Ship" pour the ancient and the modern, the
archaically primitive and the up to date, along with a wild variety
of pieces from what seem to be every society in the world.

> In the human brine of the Caribbean . . . so absorbed
> in his adventure that he didn't stop as he always did in
> front of the Hindu shops to look at the ivory mandarins
> carved of the whole tusk of an elephant, nor did he
> make fun of the Dutch Negroes in their orthopedic
> velocipedes, nor was he frightened as at other times of
> the copper-skinned Malayans who had gone around the
> world enthralled by the chimera of a secret tavern,
> where they sold roast filets of Brazillian women, because
> he wasn't aware of anything until night came over him
> with all the weight of the stars and the jungle exhaled
> a sweet fragrance of gardenias and rotten salaman-
> ders . . .

This passage illustrates how García Márquez gives dramatic
form to the unprecedented mingling of cultures and concepts of
culture that is the most significant social feature of our era. This
intermixing swamps every viable local tradition, so that the
confluence constituting the social present must be faced nakedly,
without the aid of conventions of discourse from the past though
which to mediate this new reality. García Márquez has been,
perhaps, more successful at meeting this challenge than any

other contemporary writer, and nowhere more brilliantly than in "The Ghost Ship," whose single sentence encompasses all the diversities in the passage I have just cited—and, literally, hundreds more. The story's single sentence form is not a virtuoso's trick, no flashy display of rhetorical skill for its own sake. The single sentence is essential to García Márquez' subject, which is the irresistible interpenetrating of different ways of being human, and the different products of those ways. At the postmodern instant of history, as the world plunges inevitably into cultural homogenization, it is the flowing together of cultures that dominates all social, political, economic, and therefore, aesthetic processes. It is the final flash of overlapping, intersecting, intermingling sociocultural differences disappearing into a totally cosmopolitanized mode of life (absolutely antithetical to the differentiation of ways of life on which earlier humanistic ideals were founded) that García Márquez renders so dazzlingly vivid, because he is willing even to dissolve received syntactic form, not into mere formlessness—the story is composed of a single super-sentence—but into a new conception of synthetic form not tied, to cite its most salient characteristic, to any particular language. Formally, therefore, García Márquez's story and Rabassa's translation are identical, the translation introducing no distortion at all, for it, like the original, is composed of a single sentence.

The Caribbean does, indeed, seem a perfect setting for the rendering of this flowing together of what previously had defined itself as incommensurate and incompatible. The contiguity of physical entities, "innocent parrots whose craws were full of diamonds," or orthopedic velocipedes, for example, and human *bodies*, concretize the interaction of diverse mindsets deriving from a variety of sociocultural traditions in decay, no longer able to sustain their differentiations. The fluid dramatization in a single sentence of the moving together of these decentered fragments of diverse sociocultural differentia allows "The Ghost Ship" to be extraordinarily persuasive in its contrastive representation of the very different instabilities on which depend the continuity of the natural world: "the flash of dolphins in the sea," the "lovemaking of manta rays," and "blue corvinas diving into the clear wells of softer waters," through which drift "hairs of victims of drowning in some colonial shipwreck," and where not long after we see the grounding of the "colossal" modern liner, imagining for ourselves "a crash of metal and explosion of engines" that would terrify "the soundest-sleeping dragons in the prehistoric jungle that began with the last streets of the village and ended on the other side of the world."

The essence of this confluential art is a disrupting of any structuralized understanding of phenomenona, which means that García Márquez's story challenges in a more significant way than had surrealism the predominant modern system for rationally describing reality. Such thinking finds meaning in some kind of pattern, which provides discernible form and comprehensible simplicity to what it defines as seeming discontinuities and irregularities. For García Márquez, such structures do not provide successful explanations but, to the contrary, are what most needs to be explained. Thus perhaps the most mysterious feature of the ghost ship is the regularity of its annual return. And the meaning of this system of recurrence, whatever one takes that to be, is revealed only by its disruption, by the revengeful orphan leading it off course cataclysmically to crash into the village, when, "no longer a March dawn but the noon of a radiant Wednesday," he may enjoy the villagers gaping at the impossible reality smack in the middle of their lives.

García Márquez' disruption of structuralist or pattern thinking, well illustrated by the crossing of the two temporal systems, monthly and weekly, in the phrase just cited, the crossing having the effect of canceling the authority of each, seems to me an effort to rehumanize his readers' imaginations by compelling them to respond to the overlapping of heterogeneous force-fields within which we exist. The wonderful success of the story is enabling us to share the villagers' astounding experience. That sharing, that joint participation in wonder, frees us from imprisonment within self-imposed systems of mechanized imagining which so much of modern life encourages, even dismantling the constrictive fictions of modernism. These are peculiarly sinister because they are so seductive in their limiting, confining, reducing of imagination—they do so by the very act of asserting the triumph of the human mind over the natural world.

It seems to me by no means chance that García Márquez is a New World writer and a Latin American one. He speaks for a major portion of the world that was exploited by modern Europeans as ground for developing concepts such as primitivism. In recent years such concepts have, of course, been discredited by intellectuals and scientists. The anthropologist Clifford Geertz, for instance, in discussing the "theatre state" of the Balinese points out that "the connection between what Bagehot called the dignified parts of government and the efficient ones has been systematically misconceived," and argues that understanding is crippled by the "tired commonplaces, the worn coin of European ideological debate" that allows "most of what is most interesting . . . to escape our view," and that prevents us from elaborating "a poetics of power, not a mechanics."[5] García Márquez' fiction seems to me an artistic expression of an analogous resistance to imposed conceptual systems that would deny the possibility of other, indigenous modes not merely for dealing with the world but also for conceiving what constitutes that world.

This is why García Márquez can justly be aligned less with his immediate predecessors than with the original Romantics, why, however one may wish to define his kind of "magical realism," one should keep in mind the relation of the practice to some profound Romantic commitments that, as I have tried to show, underlie their fantasy. And were one to extend the study of Romantic fantasy the affiliation would appear even stronger. Lord Byron, for instance, preached that the function of the imaginative writer was to expose the lies by which we have taught ourselves to live, to replace our conventionalized fictions that come to seem to be the only reality. What best exposes such internalized fictions are what Blake termed the "corrosive fires" of difference. But no more than Blake did Byron conceive of striking off "mind-forged manacles" as revealing some "objective truth." For the Romantics as for García Márquez, what is true and real for any human being is defined by what that human being is capable of imagining, and the potency of such reality is determined by the degree to which such imagining of it can be shared.

Because he is an artist, García Márquez' Romantic alignment is peculiarly manifested in the intensity of his concern with style. His art thus contrasts with Dunsany's relatively superficial Romanticism, revealed by his too-fluent easiness of manner. "The Ghost Ship," compared to "The Sword of Welleran," is hallucinatory, but only in the sense that Keats's "Ode to Psyche" is hallucinatory. The essential differences between Keats and García Márquez arise from the poststructuralist writer being afflicted by a more dehumanized society. He is haunted into more anguished self-consciousness, because the possibilities of productive relations with earlier forms of creativity, those deriving from, and therefore giving access to, cultural situations distinct from his own, are for him more thoroughly constricted. Keats believed, rightly, that he could remake the ballad and the ode. García Márquez must begin by remaking even the grammar of the sentence, the linguistic substratum of all literary genres. Which means that he must carry oxymoron beyond itself. The climax of "The Ghost Ship" is the appearance of a meaningless word. By thus breaking free of the supposedly enabling structure of his language, he opens a way to recovering the potency of all language, destroyed by Modernism's insidiously attractive belief that only language is real, possibly the subtlest form of modern man's self-dehumanizing. This belief, a perversion of the crucial truth that language is the most powerful of all our tools, is perverse because it makes human beings servants, not masters, of their words, thereby giving a false legitimacy to the impersonalized bureaucracies which are the plague of every twentieth-century society.

At the conclusion of "The Ghost Ship," when the liner stands, "twenty times taller than the steeple and some ninety-seven times longer than the village," with the "seas of death dripping down its sides," its name, engraved in iron letters, for the first time appears: *Halalcsillag*. The name "means nothing" in any known language, because it identifies a reality that had never before been imagined. García Márquez' ship could not appropriately bear a name meaningful in an already existent language. Yet the meaningless word's relation to what we conceive language to be is established by our immediate recognition that it is indubitably the ship's name. Once again, García

Márquez is not being superficially ingenious. Like Keats, but operating with a self-reflexivity forced on him more urgently by an environment even more hostile to fantasy than that of the Romantic era, he helps us to imagine how language, any language, could create meaning, how it might determine, not merely refer to, the nature of the reality in which we live. Unless he, and we, can thus make meaning, he is imprisoned, as we are, in the conventionalized definition of reality formed by words as normally used. As normally used, words are taken to refer simply and directly to things and actions. In normal usage the contradictory dynamism symptomatic of their potency to shape the mode of our encounters with nonverbal actualities "out there" is ignored. But it is this disregarded creative power that finally makes words, and the sentences and discourses built up of them, most useful—and therefore most dangerous—for humans living in a cosmos shared with others, with what is not human.

Today, even more than during the Napoleonic era, it is fantasy that most rapidly allows us to recover the power of thus using language creatively, to reassert our human power to overcome the strength of human creations which function to dehumanize us by confining us within reified structures of our own making. Fantasy is an enabling mode because it recovers for us a necessary sense that there is something other than ourselves for us to wonder at together. Fantasy opens the marvelous possibility of sharing an expanded sense that there may be more than us and our creations on this earth, that "more" calling forth the utmost strength of our imagining, such strength being manifested in the necessary complexities of effective human communication. To perceive this is to recognize why fantasy is a magnified development of oxymoron, because it manifests the human power to conceive the inconceivable, the inconceivable being, most simply, whatever is different from the conceiver. And only to the degree that the inconceivable can be communicated, thus becoming common property, can the potency of the truly human be enhanced.

APPENDIX 1

Æpyornis Island

H. G. WELLS

HE MAN WITH THE SCARRED FACE LEANT OVER THE table and looked at my bundle.

"Orchids?" he asked.

"A few," I said.

"Cypripediums?" he said.

"Chiefly," said I.

"Anything new?—I thought not. *I* did these islands twenty-five—twenty-seven years ago. If you find anything new here—well, it's brand new. I didn't leave much."

"I'm not a collector," said I.

"I was young then," he went on. "Lord! how I used to fly round." He seemed to take my measure. "I was in the East Indies two years, and in Brazil seven. Then I went to Madagascar."

"I know a few explorers by name," I said, anticipating a yarn. "Whom did you collect for?"

"Dawsons. I wonder if you've heard the name of Butcher ever?"

"Butcher—Butcher?" The name seemed vaguely present in my memory; then I recalled *Butcher vs. Dawson.* "Why!" said I, "you are the man who sued them for four years' salary—got cast away on a desert island . . ."

"Your servant," said the man with the scar, bowing. "Funny case wasn't it? Here was me, making a little fortune on that island, doing nothing for it neither, and them quite unable to

141

give me notice. It often used to amuse me thinking over it while I was there. I did calculations of it—big—all over the blessed atoll in ornamental figuring."

"How did it happen?" said I. "I don't rightly remember the case."

"Well . . . You've heard of the Æpyornis?"

"Rather. Andrews was telling me of a new species he was working on only a month or so ago. Just before I sailed. They've got a thigh bone, it seems, nearly a yard long. Monster the thing must have been!"

"I believe you," said the man with the scar. "It *was* a monster. Sinbad's roc was just a legend of 'em. But when did they find these bones?"

"Three or four years ago—'91, I fancy. Why?"

"Why? Because *I* found 'em—Lord!—it's nearly twenty years ago. If Dawsons hadn't been silly about that salary they might have made a perfect ring in 'em. . . . I couldn't help the infernal boat going adrift."

He paused. "I suppose it's the same place. A kind of swamp about ninety miles north of Antananarivo. Do you happen to know? You have to go to it along the coast by boats. You don't happen to remember, perhaps?"

"I don't. I fancy Andrews said something about a swamp."

"It must be the same. It's on the east coast. And somehow there's something in the water that keeps things from decaying. Like cresote it smells. It reminded me of Trinidad. Did they get any more eggs? Some of the eggs I found were a foot-and-a-half long. The swamp goes circling round, you know, and cuts off this bit. It's mostly salt, too. Well. . . . What a time I had of it! I found the things quite by accident. We went for eggs, me and two native chaps, in one of those rum canoes all tied together, and found the bones at the same time. We had a tent and provisions for four days, and we pitched on one of the firmer places. To think of it brings that odd tarry smell back even now. It's funny work. You go probing into the mud with iron rods, you know. Usually the egg gets smashed. I wonder how long it is since these Æpyornises really lived. The missionaries say the natives have legends about when they were alive, but I never heard any such

stories myself.* But certainly those eggs we got were as fresh as if
they had been new laid. Fresh! Carrying them down to the boat
one of my nigger chaps dropped one on a rock and it smashed.
How I lammed into the beggar! But sweet it was, as if it was new
laid, not even smelly, and its mother dead these four hundred
years, perhaps. Said a centipede had bit him. However, I'm
getting off the straight with the story. It had taken us all day to dig
into the slush and get these eggs out unbroken, and we were all
covered with beastly black mud, and naturally I was cross. So far
as I knew they were the only eggs that have ever been got out not
even cracked. I went afterwards to see the ones they have at the
Natural History Museum in London; all of them were cracked
and just stuck together like a mosaic, and bits missing. Mine were
perfect, and I meant to blow them when I got back. Naturally I
was annoyed at the silly duffer dropping three hours' work just on
account of a centipede. I hit him about rather."

The man with the scar took out a clay pipe. I placed my
pouch before him. He filled up absent-mindedly.

"How about the others? Did you get those home? I don't
remember——"

"That's the queer part of the story. I had three others.
Perfectly fresh eggs. Well, we put 'em in the boat, and then I
went up to the tent to make some coffee, leaving my two
heathens down by the beach—the one fooling about with his
sting and the other helping him. It never occurred to me that the
beggars would take advantage of the peculiar position I was in to
pick a quarrel. But I suppose the centipede poison and the
kicking I had given him had upset the one—he was always a
cantankerous sort—and he persuaded the other.

"I remember I was sitting and smoking and boiling up the
water over a spirit-lamp business I used to take on these expedi-
tions. Incidentally I was admiring the swamp under the sunset.
All black and blood-red it was, in streaks—a beautiful sight. And
up beyond the land rose grey and hazy to the hills, and the sky
behind them red, like a furnace mouth. And fifty yards behind

---

* No European is known to have seen a live Æpyornis, with the doubtful
exception of MacAndrew, who visited Madagascar in 1745.—H. G. W.

the back of me was these blessed heathen—quite regardless of the tranquil air of things—plotting to cut off with the boat and leave me all alone with three days provisions and a canvas tent, and nothing to drink whatsoever, beyond a little keg of water. I heard a kind of yelp behind me, and there they were in this canoe affair—it wasn't properly a boat—and, perhaps, twenty yards from land. I realised what was up in a moment. My gun was in the tent, and, besides, I had no bullets—only duck shot. They knew that. But I had a little revolver in my pocket, and I pulled that out as I ran down to the beach.

' "Come back!' says I, flourishing it.

"They jabbered something at me, and the man that broke the egg jeered. I aimed at the other—because he was unwounded and had the paddle, and I missed. They laughed. However, I wasn't beat. I knew I had to keep cool, and I tried him again and made him jump with the whang of it. He didn't laught that time. The third time I got his head, and over he went, and the paddle with him. It was a precious lucky shot for a revolver. I reckon it was fifty yards. He went right under. I don't know if he was shot, or simply stunned and drowned. Then I began to shout to the other chap to come back, but he huddled up in the canoe and refused to answer. So I fired out my revolver at him and never got near him.

"I felt a precious fool, I can tell you. There I was on this rotten, black beach, flat swamp all behind me, and the flat sea, cold after the sunset, and just this black canoe drifting steadily out to sea. I tell you I damned Dawsons and Jamrachs and Museums and all the rest of it just to rights. I bawled to this nigger to come back, until my voice went up into a scream.

"There was nothing for it but to swim after him and take my luck. So I opened my clasp-knife for convenience, and put it in my mouth, and took off my clothes and waded in. As soon as I was in the water I lost sight of the canoe, but I aimed, as I judged, to head it off. I hoped the man in it was too bad to navigate it, and that it would keep on drifting in the same direction. Presently it came up over the horizon again to the south-westward about. The afterglow of sunset was well over now and the dim of night creeping up. The stars were coming through the blue. I swum like a champion, though my legs and arms were soon aching.

"However, I came up to him by the time the stars were fairly out. As it got darker I began to see all manner of glowing things in the water—phosphorescence, you know. At times it made me giddy. I hardly knew which was stars and which was phosphorescence, and whether I was swimming on my head or my heels. The canoe was as black as sin, and the ripple under the bows like liquid fire. I was naturally chary of clambering up into it. I was anxious to see what he was up to first. He seemed to be lying cuddled up in a lump in the bows, and the stern was all out of water. The thing kept turning round slowly as it drifted—kind of waltzing, don't you know. I went to the stern and pulled it down, expecting him to wake up. Then I began to clamber in with my knife in my hand, and ready for a rush. But he never stirred. So there I sat in the stern of the little canoe, drifting away over the calm phosphorescent sea, and with all the host of star above me, waiting for something to happen.

"After a long time I called him by name, but he never answered. I was too tired to take any risks by going along to him. So we sat there. I fancy I dozed once or twice. When the dawn came I saw he was as dead as a doornail and all puffed up and purple. My three eggs and the bones were lying in the middle of the canoe, and the keg of water and some coffee and biscuits wrapped in a Cape *Argus* by his feet, and a tin of methylated spirit underneath him. There was no paddle, nor, in fact, anything except the spirit-tin that one could use as one, so I settled to drift until I was picked up. I held an inquest on him, brought in a verdict against some snake, scorpion, or centipede unknown, and sent him overboard.

"After that I had a drink of water and a few biscuits, and took a look round. I suppose a man low down as I was don't see very far; leastways, Madagascar was clean out of sight, and any trace of land at all. I saw a sail going south-westward—looked like a schooner, but her hull never came up. Presently the sun got high in the sky and began to beat down upon me. Lord! It pretty near made my brains boil. I tried dipping my head in the sea, but after a while my eye fell on the Cape *Argus*, and I lay down flat in the canoe and spread this over me. Wonderful things these newspapers! I never read one through thoroughly before, but it's odd what you get up to when you're alone, as I was. I suppose I read that blessed old Cape *Argus* twenty times. The pitch in the canoe simply reeked with the heat and rose up into big blisters.

"I drifted ten days," said the man with the scar. "It's a little thing in the telling, isn't it? Every day was like the last. Except in the morning and the evening I never kept a look-out even—the blaze was so infernal. I didn't see a sail after the first three days, and those I saw took no notice of me. About the sixth night a ship went by scarcely half a mile away from me, with all its lights ablaze and its ports open, looking like a big firefly. There was music aboard. I stood up and shouted and screamed at it. The second day I broached one of the Æpyornis eggs, scraped the shell away at the end bit by bit, and tried it, and I was glad to find it was good enough to eat. A bit flavoury—not bad, I mean—but with something of the taste of a duck's egg. There was a kind of circular patch, about six inches across, on one side of the yolk, and with streaks of blood and a white mark like a ladder in it that I thought queer, but I did not understand what this meant at the time, and I wasn't inclined to be particular. The egg lasted me three days, with biscuits and a drink of water. I chewed coffee berries too—invigorating stuff. The second egg I opened about the eighth day, and it scared me."

The man with the scar paused. "Yes," he said, "developing."

"I dare say you find it hard to believe. I did, with the thing before me. There the egg had been, sunk in that cold black mud, perhaps three hundred years. But there was no mistaking it. There was the—what is it?—embryo, with its big head and curved back, and its heart beating under its throat, and the yolk shrivelled up and great membranes spreading inside of the shell and all over the yolk. Here was I hatching out the eggs of the biggest of all extinct birds, in a little canoe in the midst of the Indian Ocean. If old Dawson had known that! It was worth four years' salary. What do *you* think?

"However, I had to eat that precious thing up, every bit of it, before I sighted the reef, and some of the mouthfuls were beastly unpleasant. I left the third one alone. I held it up to the light, but the shell was too thick for me to get any notion of what might be happening inside; and though I fancied I heard blood pulsing, it might have been the rustle in my own ears, like what you listen to in a seashell.

"Then came the atoll. Came out of the sunrise, as it were, suddenly, close up to me. I drifted straight towards it until I was about half a mile from shore, not more, and then the current took a turn, and I had to paddle as hard as I could with my hands and bits of the Æpyornis shell to make the place. However, I got there. It was just a common atoll about four miles round, with a few trees growing and a spring in one place, and the lagoon full of parrot-fish. I took the egg ashore and put it in a good place well above the tide lines and in the sun, to give it all the chance I could, and pulled the canoe up safe, and loafed about prospecting. It's rum how dull an atoll is. As soon as I had found a spring all the interest seemed to vanish. When I was a kid I thought nothing could be finer or more adventurous than the Robinson Crusoe business, but that place was as monotonous as a book of sermons. I went round finding eatable things and generally thinking; but I tell you I was bored to death before the first day was out. It shows my luck—the very day I landed the weather changed. A thunderstorm went by to the north and flicked its wing over the island, and in the night there came a drencher and a howling wind slap over us. It wouldn't have taken much, you know, to upset that canoe.

"I was sleeping under the canoe, and the egg was luckily among the sand higher up the beach, and the first thing I remember was a sound like a hundred pebbles hitting the boat at once, and a rush of water over my body. I'd been dreaming of Antananarivo, and I sat up and holloaed to Intoshi to ask her what the devil was up, and clawed out at the chair where the matches used to be. Then I remembered where I was. There was phosphorscent waves rolling up as if they meant to eat me, and all the rest of the night as black as pitch. The air was simply yelling. The clouds seemed down on your head almost, and the rain fell as if heaven was sinking and they were baling out the waters above the firmament. One great roller came writhing at me, like a fiery serpent, and I bolted. Then I thought of the canoe, and ran down to it as the water went hissing back again; but the thing had gone. I wondered about the egg then, and felt my way to it. It was all right and well out of reach of the maddest waves, so I sat down beside it and cuddled it for company. Lord! what a night that was!

"The storm was over before the morning. There wasn't a rag of cloud left in the sky when the dawn came, and all along the beach there were bits of plank scattered—which was the disarticulated skeleton, so to speak, of my canoe. However, that gave me something to do, for, taking advantage of two of the trees being together, I rigged up a kind of storm-shelter with these vestiges. And that day the egg hatched.

"Hatched, sir, when my head was pillowed on it and I was asleep. I heard a whack and felt a jar and sat up, and there was the end of the egg pecked out and a rum little brown head looking out at me. 'Lord!' I said, 'you're welcome'; and with a little difficulty he came out.

"He was a nice friendly little chap at first, about the size of a small hen—very much like most other young birds, only bigger. His plumage was a dirty brown to begin with, with a sort of grey scab that fell off it very soon, and scarcely feathers—a kind of downy hair. I can hardly express how pleased I was to see him. I tell you, Robinson Crusoe don't make near enough of his loneliness. But here was interesting company. He looked at me and winked his eye from the front backwards, like a hen, and gave a chirp and began to peck about at once, as though being hatched three hundred years too late was just nothing. 'Glad to see you, Man Friday!' says I, for I had naturally settled he was to be called Man Friday if ever he was hatched, as soon as ever I found the egg in the canoe had developed. I was a bit anxious about his feed, so I gave him a lump of raw parrot-fish at once. He took it, and opened his beak for more. I was glad of that, for, under the circumstances, if he'd been at all fanciful I should have had to eat him after all.

"You'd be surprised what an interesting bird that Æpyornis chick was. He followed me about from the very beginning. He used to stand by me and watch while I fished in the lagoon, and go shares in anything I caught. And he was sensible, too. There were nasty green warty things, like pickled gherkins, used to lie about on the beach, and he tried one of these and it upset him. He never even looked at any of them again.

"And he grew. You could almost see him grow. And as I was never much of a society man his quiet, friendly ways suited me to a T. For nearly two years we were as happy as we could be on that island. I had no business worries, for I knew my salary was mounting up at Dawsons'. We would see a sail now and then, but nothing ever came near us. I amused myself, too, by decorating the island with designs worked in sea-urchins and fancy shells of various kinds. I put ÆPYORNIS ISLAND all round the place very nearly, in big letters, like what you see done with coloured stones at railway stations in the old country, and mathematical calculations and drawings of various sorts. And I used to lie watching the blessed bird stalking round and growing, growing; and think how I could make a living out of him by showing him about if I ever got taken off. After his first moult he began to get handsome, with a crest and a blue wattle, and a lot of green feathers at the behind of him. And then I used to puzzle whether Dawsons had any right to claim him or not. Stormy weather and in the rainy season we lay snug under the shelter I had made out of the old canoe, and I used to tell him lies about my friends at home. And after a storm we would go round the island together to see if there was any drift. It was a kind of idyll, you might say. If only I had had some tobacco it would have been simply just like Heaven.

"It was about the end of the second year our little paradise went wrong. Friday was then about fourteen feet high to the bill of him, with a big, broad head like the end of a pickaxe, and two huge brown eyes with yellow rims, set together like a man's—not out of sight of each other like a hen's. His plumage was fine—none of the half-mourning style of your ostrich—more like a cassowary as far as colour and texture goes. And then it was he began to cock his comb at me and give himself airs, and show signs of a nasty temper. . . .

"At last came a time when my fishing had been rather unlucky, and he began to hang about me in a queer, meditative way. I thought he might have been eating sea-cucumbers or something, but it was really just discontent on his part. I was hungry, too, and when at last I landed a fish I wanted it for myself. Tempers were short that morning on both sides. He pecked at it and grabbed it, and I gave him a whack on the head to make him leave go. And at that he went for me. Lord! . . .

"He gave me this in the face" The man indicated his scar. "Then he kicked me. It was like a cart-horse. I got up, and seeing he hadn't finished, I started off full tilt with my arms doubled up over my face. But he ran on those gawky legs of his faster than a racehorse, and kept landing out at me with sledge-hammer kicks, and bringing his pickaxe down on the back of my head. I made for the lagoon, and went in up to my neck. He stopped at the water, for he hated getting his feet wet, and began to make a shindy, something like a peacock's, only hoarser. He started strutting up and down the beach. I'll admit I felt small to see this blessed fossil lording it there. And my head and face were all bleeding, and—well, my body just one jelly of bruises.

"I decided to swim across the lagoon and leave him alone for a bit until the affair blew over. I shinned up the tallest palm-tree, and sat there thinking of it all. I don't suppose I ever felt so hurt by anything before or since. It was the brutal ingratitude of the creature. I'd been more than a brother to him. I'd hatched him, educated him. A great gawky, out-of-date bird! And me a human being—heir of the ages and all of it.

"I thought after a time he'd begin to see things in that light himself, and feel a little sorry for his behaviour. I thought if I was to catch some nice little bits of fish, perhaps, and go to him presently in a casual kind of way, and offer them to him, he might do the sensible thing. It took me some time to learn how unforgiving and cantankerous an extinct bird can be. Malice!

"I won't tell you all the little devices I tried to get that bird round again. I simply can't. It makes my cheek burn with shame even now to think of the snubs and buffets I had from this infernal curiosity. I tried violence. I chucked lumps of coral at him from a safe distance, but he only swallowed them. I shied my open knife at him and almost lost it, though it was too big for him to swallow. I tried starving him out and struck fishing, but he took to picking along the beach at low water after worms, and rubbed along on that. Half my time I spent up to my neck in the lagoon, and the rest up the palm-trees. One of them was scarcely high enough, and when he caught me up it he had a regular Bank Holiday with the calves of my legs. It got unbearable. I don't know if you have ever tried sleeping up a palm-tree. It gave me the most horrible nightmares. Think of the shame of it, too! Here was this extinct animal mooning about my island like a sulky duke, and me not allowed to rest the sole of my foot on the place. I used to cry with weariness and vexation. I told him straight that I didn't mean to be chased about a desert island by any damned anachronisms. I told him to go and peck a navigator of his own age. But he only snapped his beak at me. Great ugly bird—all legs and neck.!

"I shouldn't like to say how long that went on altogether. I'd have killed him sooner if I'd known how. However, I hit on a way of settling him at last. It is a South American dodge. I joined all my fishing-lines together with stems of seaweed and things and made a stoutish string, perhaps twelve yards in length or more, and I fastened two lumps of coral rock to the ends of this. It took me some time to do, because every now and then I had to go into the lagoon or up a tree as the fancy took me. This I whirled rapidly round my head, and then let it go at him. The first time I missed, but the next time the string caught his legs beautifully, and wrapped round them again and again. Over he went. I threw it standing waist-deep in the lagoon, and as soon as he went down I was out of the water and sawing at his neck with my knife . . .

"I don't like to think of that even now. I felt like a murderer while I did it, though my anger was hot against him. When I stood over him and saw him bleeding on the white sand, and his beautiful great legs and neck writhing in his last agony . . . Pah!

"With that tragedy loneliness came upon me like a curse. Good Lord! you can't imagine how I missed that bird. I sat by his corpse and sorrowed over him, and shivered as I looked round the desolate, silent reef. I thought of what a jolly little bird he had been when he was hatched, and of a thousand pleasant tricks he had played before he went wrong. I thought if I'd only wounded him I might have nursed him round into a better understanding. If I'd had any means of digging into the coral rock I'd have buried him. I felt exactly as if he was human. As it was, I couldn't think of eating him, so I put him in the lagoon, and the little fishes picked him clean. I didn't even save the feathers. Then one day a chap cruising about in a yacht had a fancy to see if my atoll still existed.

"He didn't come a moment too soon, for I was about sick enough of the desolation of it, and only hesitating whether I should walk out into the sea and finish up the business that way, or fall back on the green things. . . .

"I sold the bones to a man named Winslow—a dealer near the British Museum, and he says he sold them to old Havers. It seems Havers didn't understand they were extra large, and it was only after his death they attracted attention. They called 'em Æpyornis—what was it?"

"*Æpyornis vastus*," said I. "It's funny, the very thing was mentioned to me by a friend of mine. When they found an Æpyornis, with a thigh a yard long, they thought they had reached the top of the scale, and called him *Æpyornis maximus*. Then someone turned up another thigh-bone four feet six or more, and that they called *Æpyornis Titan*. Then your *vastus* was found after old Havers died, in his collection, and then a *vastissimus* turned up."

"Winslow was telling me as much," said the man with the scar. "If they get any more Æpyornises, he reckons some scientific swell will go and burst a blood-vessel. But it was a queer thing to happen to a man; wasn't it—altogether?"

The Last Voyage of the Ghost Ship

GABRIEL GARCÍA MÁRQUEZ

OW THEY'RE GOING TO SEE WHO I AM, HE SAID TO himself in his strong new man's voice, many years after he had first seen the huge ocean liner without lights and without any sound which passed by the village one night like a great uninhabited palace, longer than the whole village and much taller than the steeple of the church, and it sailed by in the darkness toward the colonial city on the other side of the bay that had been fortified against buccaneers, with its old slave port and the rotating light, whose gloomy beams transfigured the village into a lunar encampment of glowing houses and streets of volcanic deserts every fifteen seconds, and even though at that time he'd been a boy without a man's strong voice but with his mother's permission to stay very late on the beach to listen to the wind's night harps, he could still remember, as if still seeing it, how the liner would disappear when the light of the beacon struck its side and how it would reappear when the light had passed, so that it was an intermittent ship sailing along, appearing and disappearing, toward the mouth of the bay, groping its way like a sleepwalker for the buoys that marked the harbor channel until something must have gone wrong with the compass needle, because it headed toward the shoals, ran aground, broke up, and sank without a single sound, even though a collision against the reefs like that should have

153

produced a crash of metal and the explosion of engines that
would have frozen with fright the soundest-sleeping dragons in
the prehistoric jungle that began with the last streets of the village
and ended on the other side of the world, so that he himself
thought it was a dream, especially the next day, when he saw the
radiant fishbowl of the bay, the disorder of colors of the Negro
shacks on the hills above the harbor, the schooners of the
smugglers from the Guianas loading their cargoes of innocent
parrots whose craws were full of diamonds, he thought, I fell
asleep counting the stars and I dreamed about that huge ship, of
course, he was so convinced that he didn't tell anyone nor did he
remember the vision again until the same night on the following
March when he was looking for the flash of dolphins in the sea
and what he found was the illusory liner, gloomy, intermittent,
with the same mistaken direction as the first time, except that
then he was so sure he was awake that he ran to tell his mother
and she spent three weeks moaning with disappointment, because your brain's rotting away from doing so many things
backward, sleeping during the day and going out at night like a
criminal, and since she had to go to the city around that time to
get something comfortable where she could sit and think about
her dead husband, because the rockers on her chair had worn
out after eleven years of widowhood, she took advantage of the
occasion and had the boatman go near the shoals so that her
son could see what he really saw in the glass of the sea, the
lovemaking of manta rays in a spring-time of sponges, pink
snappers and blue corvinas diving into the other wells of softer
waters that were there among the waters, and even the wandering hairs of victims of drowning in some colonial shipwreck, no
trace of sunken liners or anything like it, and yet he was so
pigheaded that his mother promised to watch with him the next
March, absolutely, not knowing that the only thing absolute in
her future now was an easy chair from the days of Sir Francis
Drake which she had bought at an auction in a Turk's store, in
which she sat down to rest that same night, sighing, oh, my poor
Olofernos, if you could only see how nice it is to think about you
on this velvet lining and this brocade from the casket of a queen,
but the more she brought back the memory of her dead husband,

the more the blood in her heart bubbled up and turned to chocolate, as if instead of sitting down she were running, soaked from chills and fevers and her breathing full of earth, until he returned at dawn and found her dead in the easy chair, still warm, but half rotted away as after a snakebite, the same as happened afterward to four other women before the murderous chair was thrown into the sea, far away where it wouldn't bring evil to anyone, because it had been used so much over the centuries that its faculty for giving rest had been used up, and so he had to grow accustomed to his miserable routine of an orphan who was pointed out by everyone as the son of the widow who had brought the throne of misfortune into the village, living not so much from public charity as from the fish he stole out of boats, while his voice was becoming a roar, and not remembering his visions of past times anymore until another night in March when he chanced to look seaward and suddenly, good Lord, there it is, the huge asbestos whale, the behemoth beast, come see it, he shouted madly, come see it, raising such an uproar of dogs' barking and women's panic that even the oldest men remembered the frights of their great-grandfathers and crawled under their beds, thinking that William Dampier had come back, but those who ran into the street didn't make the effort to see the unlikely apparatus which at that instant was lost again in the east and raised up in its annual disaster, but they covered him with blows and left him so twisted that it was then he said to himself, drooling with rage, now they're going to see who I am, but he took care not to share his determination with anyone, but spent the whole year with the fixed idea, now they're going to see who I am, waiting for it to be the eve of the apparition once more in order to do what he did, which was steal a boat, cross the bay, and spend the evening waiting for his great moment in the inlets of the slave port, in the human brine of the Caribbean, but so absorbed in his adventure that he didn't stop as he always did in front of the Hindu shops to look at the ivory mandarins carved from the whole tusk of an elephant, nor did he make fun of the Dutch Negroes in their orthopedic velocipedes, nor was he frightened as at other times of the copper-skinned Malayans, who had gone around the world enthralled by the chimera of a secret tavern where they sold roast filets of Brazilian women, because he wasn't aware of anything until night came over him with all the weight of the stars and the jungle exhaled a sweet fragrance of gardenias and rotten salamanders, and there he was, rowing in the stolen boat toward the mouth of the bay, with the lantern out so as not to alert the customs police, idealized every fifteen seconds by the green wing flap of the beacon and turned human once more by the darkness, knowing that he was getting close to the buoys that marked the harbor channel, not only because its oppressive glow was getting more intense, but because the breathing of the water was becoming sad, and he rowed like that, so wrapped up in himself, that he didn't know where the fearful shark's breath that suddenly reached him came from or why the night became dense, as if the stars had suddenly died, and it was because the liner was there, with all of it inconceivable size, Lord, bigger than any other big thing in the world and darker than any other dark thing on land or sea, three hundred thousand tons of shark smell passing so close to the boat that he could see the seams of the steel precipice, without a single light in the infinite portholes, without a sigh from the engines, without a soul, and carrying its own circle of silence with it, its own dead air, its halted time, its errant sea in which a whole world of drowned animals floated, and suddenly it all disappeared with the flash of the beacon and for an instant it was the diaphanous Caribbean once more, the March night, the everyday air of the pelicans, so he stayed alone among the buoys, not knowing what to do, asking himself, startled, if perhaps he wasn't dreaming while he was awake, not just now but the other times too, but no sooner had he asked himself than a breath of mystery snuffed out the buoys, from the first to the last, so that when the light of the beacon passed by the liner appeared again and now its compasses were out of order, perhaps not even knowing what part of the ocean sea it was in, groping for the invisible channel but actually heading for the shoals, until he got the overwhelming revelation that that misfortune of the buoys was the last key to the enchantment and he lighted the lantern in the boat, a tiny red light that had no reason to alarm anyone in the watchtowers but which would be like a guiding sun for the pilot, because, thanks

to it, the liner corrected its course and passed into the main gate
of the channel in a maneuver of lucky resurrection, and then all
the lights went on at the same time so that the boilers wheezed
again, the stars were fixed in their places, and the animal corpses
went to the bottom, and there was a clatter of plates and a
fragrance of laurel sauce in the kitchens, and one could hear the
pulsing of the orchestra on the moon decks and the throbbing of
the arteries of high-sea lovers in the shadows of the staterooms,
but he still carried so much leftover rage in him that he would not
let himself be confused by emotion or be frightened by the
miracle, but said to himself with more decision than ever, now
they're going to see who I am, the cowards, now they're going to
see, and instead of turning aside so that the colossal machine
would not charge into him, he began to row in front of it,
because now they really are going to see who I am, and he
continued guiding the ship with the lantern until he was so sure
of its obedience that he made it change course from the direction
of the docks once more, took it out of the invisible channel, and
led it by the halter as if it were a sea lamb toward the lights of the
sleeping village, a living ship, invulnerable to the torches of the
beacon, that no longer made it invisible but made it aluminum
every fifteen seconds, and the crosses of the church, the misery
of the houses, the illusion began to stand out, and still the ocean
liner followed behind him, following his will inside of it, the
captain asleep on his heart side, the fighting bulls in the snow of
their pantries, the solitary patient in the infirmary, the orphan
water of its cisterns, the unredeemed pilot who must have
mistaken the cliffs for the docks, because at that instant the great
roar of the whistle burst forth, once, and he was soaked with the
downpour of steam that fell on him, again, and the boat
belonging to someone else was on the point of capsizing, and
again, but it was too late, because there were the shells of the
shoreline, the stones of the streets, the doors of the disbelievers,
the whole village illuminated by the lights of the fearsome liner
itself, and he barely had time to get out of the way to make room
for the cataclysm, shouting in the midst of the confusion, there it
is, you cowards, a second before the huge steel cask shattered the
ground and one could hear the neat destruction of ninety

thousand five hundred champagne glasses breaking, one after the other, from stem to stern, and then the light came out and it was no longer a March dawn but the noon of a radiant Wednesday, and he was able to give himself the pleasure of watching the disbelievers as with open mouths they contemplated the largest ocean liner in this world and the other aground in front of the church, whiter than anything, twenty times taller than the steeple and some ninety-seven times longer than the village, with its name engraved in iron letters, *Halalcsillag*, and the ancient and languid waters of the seas of death dripping down its sides.

Notes

1 Tolkien's expansion of his Andrew Lang Lecture, "On Fairy Tales," at the University of St. Andrews in 1938 appeared in *Essays Presented to Charles Williams* (London: Oxford University Press, 1947), and is accessible in *The Tolkien Reader* (New York: Ballantine, 1966), 3–84, from which all my citations are drawn. For Tolkien, fantasy (which for him as for me encompasses the fantastic) "does not destroy or even insult Reason; and it does not blunt the appetite for, nor obscure the perception of scientific verity. On the contrary. The keener and clearer the reason, the better fantasy it will make. . . . For creative Fantasy is founded upon the hard recognition that things are so in the world" (54–55).

Tolkien emphasizes that a fairy story must be presented as true though dealing with marvels (hence its character as a form of oxymoron): "it cannot tolerate any frame or machinery suggesting that the whole story . . . is a figment or illusion" (14). This carries to the crux of his understanding of traditional fairy stories as "not primarily concerned with possibility, but with desirability" (40). For Tolkien, it is to "enchantment Fantasy aspires . . ., it does not seek delusion nor bewitchment and domination; it seeks *shared* enrichment, *partners* in making and delight" (53). The emphases I have added to his words show how his description tends toward reader-response criticism, which, as Siebers has observed (see note 3 below) makes possible efficacious analyses of literary fantasy.

2 Jean Paul Sartre, *Situations I* (Paris: Gallimard, 1947), 60; I cite the translation of Rosemary Jackson, *Fantasy, The Literature of Subversion* (London: Methuen, 1981), 18.

3 Tzvetan Todorov, *The Fantastic: A Structural Approach to a Literary Genre*, trans. Richard Howard (Cleveland: Case-Western Reserve University Press, 1973), 41. Todorov's book originally appeared under the title of *Introduction à la littérature fantastique* (Paris: Seuil, 1970). More than seems to have been realized by American critics, Todorov builds on a substantial French tradition of analysis of fantasy, for example, the excellent book of Louis Vax, *La Séduction de l'étrange* (Paris: Press Universitaires de France, 1965). Vax observes, for example, "La fantastique est un moment de crise" (149), and "le fantastique est . . . un moment de passage, de crise et de malaise" (243).

Characteristic of much criticism of Todorov's work is that of Christine Brooke-Rose in *A Rhetoric of the Unreal* (Cambridge: Cambridge University Press, 1981). She points out that when treating a writer such as Kafka, Todorov abandons his own theory, since it applies "only to the nineteenth-century texts . . . a particular genre with a short life" (67). Yet she concludes the chapter by accepting Todorov's system as a "useful working hypothesis" (71), and in fact she does little to improve on Todorov's definitions. It is difficult for her to go beyond Todorov, because her commitment to formalist and Freudian premises. Were she to submit these to analytic scrutiny, she would see the problem of the fantastic is involved in the inseparability of the conceptions of natural and supernatural she has inherited. It is this insight on which Tobin Siebers, *The Romantic Fantastic* (Ithaca: Cornell University Press, 1984), founds his critique of Todorov, whom he perceives as following the "structuralist tradition" exemplified by Levi-Strauss, who eliminates questions "of the sacred in favor of relational analysis" (35). A cogent discussion of the limitations of Todorov's approach will be found in Irène Bessière, *Le Récit fantastique: la poétique de l'incertain* (Paris: Larousse, 1974), 54–59—one of the best books on the subject, relied on heavily by Jackson and Brooke-Rose.

4 Theodore Ziolkowski, *Disenchanted Images: A Literary Iconology* (Princeton: Princeton University Press, 1977).

5 C. N. Manlove, *Modern Fantasy: Five Studies* Cambridge: Cambridge University Press, 1975), 1. Manlove makes good use of the better French critics, such as Vax, but is especially valuable for his discrimination of fantasy from science fiction, in which "otherness is never present, however remote the location" (3). An "amplification" by Manlove of his introduction to *Modern Fantasy* appears

in *The Aesthetics of Fantasy: Literature and Art*, ed. Roger C. Schlobin (Notre Dame: University of Notre Dame Press, 1982). Following the same Tolkienian line is Ann Swinfer, *In Defense of Fantasy* (London: Routledge and Kegan Paul, 1984), an excellent work particularly good at showing that Tolkien does not follow Coleridge's separation of imagination and fancy, as has sometimes been assumed, rightly suggesting that Tolkien's position is finally closer to Shelley's as articulated in *A Defence of Poetry* (see Swinfer, 7–10).

6   Rosemary Jackson, *Fantasy, The Literature of Subversion* (London: Methuen, 1981), 23. William R. Irwin's book is *The Game of the Impossible* (Urbana: University of Illinois Press, 1976), and Joanna Russ' fine article is "The Subjunctivity of Science Fiction," *Extrapolation* 15, 1, 51–59. Jackson following Bakhtin's line of argument that "modern fantasy is severed from its roots in carnivalesque art: it is not longer a communal form" (16), nonetheless relies more on Bessière's description of antinomical structure as the formal determinant of fantasy to reach her conclusion that "the basic trope of fantasy is *oxymoron*, a figure of speech which holds together contradictions and sustains them in an impossible unity, without progressing toward synthesis" (21).

7   Tobin Siebers, *The Romantic Fantastic* (Ithaca: Cornell University Press, 1985), 21–32. Siebers' earlier book, *The Mirror of Medusa* (Berkeley: University of California Press, 1983), also has relevance to material I deal with here, his focus on the evil eye being specially germane to "The Ancient Mariner," and his discussion of Freud's "Uncanny" (110–140), skillfully defines the role of that essay in Freud's development. Kathyrn Hume, *Fantasy and Mimesis* (New York: Methuen, 1984), provides a good survey of earlier criticism.

8   Siebers, 35. Vax, observing that "La littérature fantastique moderne s'est édifée sur les ruines de la vieille crédulité" (239), and that the "fantastique signifie irruption de désordre, de trouble, de folie dans un univers ordonné, serein, rationnel" (243), puts the point succinctly: "La littérature fantastique moderne est née de l'incredulité" (244).

CHAPTER 2

1   Claudio Guillen, *Literature as System* (Cambridge, Mass.: Harvard University Press, 1971) deals incisively with the impurity of literary genres.

2   Patrick Parrinder, "Science Fiction and the Scientific World View,"
     Science Fiction: Its Criticism and Teaching, ed. Patrick Parrinder
     (London: Methuen, 1980), 67–88, treats this matter, and in so doing
     quotes the now legendary John W. Campbell: "To be science
     fiction, not fantasy, an honest effort at prophetic extrapolation must
     be made" (76). Probably the most intense and intellectually ambi-
     tious of science fiction specialists is the Marxian Darko Suvin,
     whose major work is *Metamorphoses of Science Fiction* (New Haven:
     Yale University Press, 1979). Less daunting and a good introduction
     to his approach is "Narrative Logic, Ideology, and the Range of
     Science Fiction," *Science-Fiction Studies* 9, 1 (1982): 1–25, and his
     essay in the volume he edited with Robert M. Phelen, *H. G. Wells
     and Modern Science Fiction* (Lewisburg, Penn.: Bucknell University
     Press, 1977). Suvin's grasp of the history of the genre is well
     displayed in his essay "Victorian Science Fiction, 1871–85: The Rise
     of the Alternative History Sub-genre," *Science-Fiction Studies* 10, 2
     (1983): 148–65). This essay is a useful corrective to some of the
     superifical surveys mentioned below. Simpler and intellectually less
     aspiring, Patrick Parrinder is responsible for two useful volumes, the
     one cited above and *Science Fiction: A Critical Guide* (London:
     Longmans, 1979). Kingsley Amis, *New Maps of Hell: A Survey of
     Science Fiction* (New York: Harcourt, Brace, 1960) is now only of
     historical interest. Brian W. Aldiss, *Billion Year Spree* (New York:
     Schocken, 1973) is a kind of compendium written with verve and
     intelligence. Other popular surveys include Robert Scholes and
     Eric S. Rabkin, *Science Fiction* (New York: Oxford, 1977), and
     Scholes' *Structural Fabulation* (Notre Dame: University of Notre
     Dame Press, 1975), along with Leslie Fiedler's anthology with
     commentaries, *In Dreams Awake* (New York: Dell, 1975). Two
     journals, *Extrapolation: A Journal of Science Fiction and Fantasy*
     and *Science-Fiction Studies* have for some years published a high
     percentage of the best criticism and scholarship in the field.

3   J. P. Vernier, "Evolution as a Literary Theme in H. G. Wells'
     Science Fiction," in Suvin and Phelan, 70–82, quotes Wells's
     observation of his use of "material based on extrapolation": "The
     value of the story to me lies in this, that from the first to last there is
     nothing in it that is impossible" (72).

4   Scholes and Rabkin speak of "The First Century A. F. (After
     Frankenstein)" (7). See also Christopher Pries, "British Science
     Fiction" in *Science Fiction: A Critical Guide*, ed. Parrinder: "The
     first literary work which was indisputably a science fiction novel in
     the modern sense was Shelley's *Frankenstein*" (187).

5   All citations of extended passages from *Beowulf* are from the verse
    translation by Michael Alexander (Harmondsworth: Penguin, 1973)
    with page references given in my text. For the original I have used
    Beowulf and the Fight at Finnsburg, 3d ed., ed. Frederik Klaeber
    (Boston: Heath, 1950), which provides my citations by line number.
    I am grateful to my colleagues David Yerkes and Richard Sacks for
    their help in understanding the poem.
6   Arthur Brodeur, *The Art of Beowulf* (Berkeley: University of Califor-
    nia Press, 1959), 188–89, is rather hostile to comparisons with
    Ragnarok, but for other views see Paul B. Taylor, "Heorot, Earth,
    and Asgard: Christian Poetry and Pagan Myth," *Tennessee Studies
    in Literature* 11 (1966): 119–30, Ursula Drake, "Beowulf and Ragna-
    rok," *Saga-Book of the Viking Society* 17 (1969–70): 302–25, and
    Daniel G. Calder, "Setting and Ethos: The Pattern of Measure and
    Limit in *Beowulf*," *Studies in Philology* 69 (1972). For the mythical
    background, one many consult John Stanley Martin, *Ragnarok: An
    Investigation into Old Norse Concepts of the Fate of the Gods*
    (Assen: Van Gorcum, 1972).
7   Brodeur, 76.
8   Aldous Huxley, Literature and Science (New York: Harper and
    Row, 1963), 12. A *locus classicus* for this distinction is René Wellek
    and Austin Warren, *Theory of Literature*, 3d ed. (New York:
    Harcourt Brace Jovanovich, 1975 [1942]), 22–23.
9   Parrinder (1980), 108.
10 Here and throughout the chapter I cite from the New American
    Library edition of *Frankenstein*, ed. Harold Bloom (New York,
    1963), simply because it is the most easily available; its text is that of
    the third edition, published by Collum and Bentley in London in
    1831, this being the most often reprinted text. There are significant
    differences between this edition and the first of 1818, for which
    James Rieger's modern edition is useful (Indianapolis: Bobbs-
    Merrill, 1974). Changes between the first and third editions, which
    Reiger discusses at length, even the shift in the relation of Victor
    and Elizabeth, in no way disturbs my evaluations of the Franken-
    stein family and its behavior. E. B. Murray, "Shelley's Contribu-
    tions to Mary's *Frankenstein*," *Bulletin of the Keats-Shelley Memo-
    rial Association* 29 (1978): 50–68, provides the most thorough
    analysis of Percy's effect on the 1818 text—the preface to that
    edition, of course, being entirely his work.
11 Harold Bloom, "Afterword," *Frankenstein* (1963), 213. Critics such
    as Sandra Gilbert and Susan Gubar, *The Madwoman in the Attic*
    (New Haven: Yale University Press, 1979), 221, who emphasize the

literariness of *Frankenstein* by treating it as a rewriting of *Paradise Lost* in fact attentuate the cogent severity of Mary Shelley's social criticism.

12   The pervasive contemporary psychological explanation of Victor is paralleled by adulation of the monster unjustified by Mary Shelley's text. Not only is the creature's self-representation suspect for its Rousseauvian sentimentality, but the monster perpetrates three brutal murders, even gratutitously implicating Justine in William's killing. Larry J. Swingle is almost alone among modern commentators in recognizing that Shelley has constructed a novel out of self-justifying narrations whose absolute truth or falsity is indeterminable: see his "Frankenstein's Monster and Its Romantic Relatives: Problems of Knowledge in English Romanticism," *Texas Studies in Literature and Langauge* 15, 1 (1973): 51–65.

13   Even the subtitle of Shelley's novel, "A Modern Prometheus," may suggest a question as to the moral value of appealing to the good of our species. Mary's husband thought any sort of reconciliation between Prometheus and Zeus abominable, since for him there was little admirable about Zeus, whom he even called Jupiter. Aeschylus, a better playwright, felt otherwise, perhaps because for the Greeks Zeus, unlike the god of the Old Testament, was not responsible for the creation of mankind. He thought he could produce something better; from Zeus's point of view, Prometheus interfered with progress. David Ketterer, *Frankenstein's Creation: The Book, The Monster, and Human Reality*, English Literary Studies of the University of Victoria 16 (Vancouver: University of Victoria, 1979), 19–20, discusses the double mythology of Prometheus *pyrophoros* and *plasticator*.

14   This among other uses and misuses of the Frankenstein reference by modern scientists are cited by Theodore Ziolkowski in "Science, Frankenstein, and Myth," *Sewanee Review* 89, 1 (1981): 34–56.

15   Walter J. Ong, *Orality and Literacy*, (New York: Methuen, 1982), has much to say of relevance to this point, for example, his observations on "orality, community, and the social" (74–75), leading to a discussion in the following pages as to why the spoken word is not a sign.

16   Thoughtful critics of science fiction such as Suvin and Parrinder have observed this linkage and illustrated it cogently, as has Scott Sanders in "The Disappearance of Character in Science Fiction," in *Science Fiction: A Critical Guide*, ed. Parrinder, 131–49, noting science fiction is "a dialectical extension of realism," and "modern" in that it sides with Henry James in his objections to R. L.

Stevenson's "romances" (146). Mainstream critics such as Scholes and George Levine who have taken up science fiction have not adequately emphasized this connection of the genre to realism. Levine in "The Ambiguous Heritage of *Frankenstein*" in the volume edited by him and U. C. Knoepflmacher, *The Endurance of Frankenstein* (Berkeley: University of California Press, 1979), for example, argues that the nineteenth-century novel "seriously rejected the kinds of excess that make the very substance of *Frankenstein*" while admitting that several nineteenth-century novels are "a kind of mirror image of Mary Shelley's story" (21). On the whole, feminist critics such as Judith Wilt and Ellen Moers, both with essays in the volume edited by Levine and Knoepflmacher, and Mary Poovey in *The Proper Lady and the Woman Writer* (Chicago: University of Chicago Press, 1984) are more perspicuous in recognizing the relation of Shelley's novel to realistic fiction.

17 John Reider, "Embracing the Alien: Science Fiction in Mass Culture," *Science-Fiction Studies* 91 (1982): 26–37, develops this point to show that science fiction is an accessory of leisure, "linked to social conditions in which freedom shrinks into the negative and exclusionary enjoyments of privacy" (26).

18 Although Fredric Jameson, "Progress Versus Utopia," *Science-Fiction Studies* 9, 2 (1982): 147–58, simply takes Wells's position for granted, (see 149), Wells's scientific romances, and the *Time Machine* in particular, have been carefully studied. Bernard Bergonzi, *The Early H. G. Wells* (Toronto: University of Toronto Press, 1961), for instance, has analyzed the relation between *The Time Machine* and *The Chronic Argonauts*, published in 1888. Suvin, who has taken the trouble to learn much both about Wells's literary forerunners in England and about Wells's view of Huxley and Darwin, is ponderous but useful both on *The Time Machine*'s paradigmatic role for twentieth-century science fiction and on the nature of Wells's "imitation" of the scientific forms (*The Metamorphoses of Science Fiction*, chaps. 9 and 10). Suvin adds to this earlier description of how exactly Wells contributed to the evolution of science fiction in the essay "Narrative Logic, Ideology, and the Range of Science Fiction" cited above. The best book on Wells I've found is John Huntington, *The Logic of Fantasy: H. G. Wells and Science Fiction* (New York: Columbia University Press, 1982), especially helpful in defining Wells's relation to Darwin (8–15). Parrinder in *Science Fiction: A Critical Guide*, 69, is cogent on evolution and the second law of thermodynamics.

19 The view that the "real" is "reiterable" was more prevalent in the

early years of the modern era, when most scientific endeavor was more crudely positivistic than it is today.

20   Aldiss, 26, emphasizes the influence on Mary Shelley of Erasmus Darwin, whose evolutionary views in several respects anticipated those of his grandson Charles. Ketterer, 25, cites even more evidence, including entries in Mary's journal. The essay by Laura E. Crouch, "Davy's A *Discourse, Introductory to a Course of Lectures on Chemistry: A Possible Scientific Source of* Franken-stein," *Keats-Shelley Journal* 27 (1978): 35–44, is persuasive in its suggestion of Mary's knowledge of Humphrey Davy's popularizing work, which supports the idea of her sensitivity to central tendencies of the science of her day, a sensitivity that would have been encouraged by her husband

21   The "extraneousness" of the travel beyond the year 802,701 has rightly been seen as critically pivotal by the best commentators, all of whom recognize the conjunction in it of an editorial and a scientific crux. The issues it raises are too complex to explore here, since they necessarily engage one in problems of Wells's intellectual development, but an interested reader should consult the documents and commentaries in *H. G. Wells: Early Writings in Science and Science Fiction*, edited with critical commentary and notes by Robert M. Philmus and David Y. Hughes (Berkeley: University of California Press, 1975), esp. 5–11 and 49–55. Illustrative of the ambiance in which Wells's scientific thinking developed is the following from T. H. Huxley's *Evolution and Ethics*, published in 1893:

> The theory of evolution encourages no millenial anticipa-tions. If, for millions of years, our globe has taken the upward road, yet some time, the summit will be realized, and the downward road will be commenced. (T. H. Huxley and Julian Huxley, *Evolution and Ethics, 1893–1943* [Lon-don: Methuen, 1947], 83)

It is in part because the story displays Wells's understanding of various kinds of implications in evolutionary ideas (as well as illustrating the reportorial style of science fiction), that I have included in an appendix his "Æpyornis Island" as a science fiction contrast to García Márquez' "The Last Voyage of the Ghost Ship."

22   The most thoughtful analysis of this characteristic is that of Scott Sanders in Parrinder, 131–49. Sanders describes "science fiction as a genre . . . centrally about the disappearance of character" (131), and demonstrates how individuals without any need of society

constitute the "central predicament of characters in science fiction" (145).

CHAPTER 3

1   Michael Polanyi, *The Tacit Dimension* (Garden City, N.Y.: Anchor-Doubleday, 1967), 3–4.

2   *Biographia Literaria*, ed. J. Shawcross, 2 vols. (London: Oxford University Press, 1907 [1962], 2: 5–6. Mark L. Reed's persuasive argument that Coleridge's account is to a considerable degree a product of retrospective imagining, "Wordsworth, Coleridge, and the 'Plan' of the *Lyrical Ballads*, " *University of Toronto Quarterly* 34 (1965): 238–53, supports a reading of Coleridgean-Keatsian fantasy as partly subconscious opposition to Wordsworthian "naturalism." On the facts surrounding the original publication of *Lyrical Ballads*, consult John Jordan, *Why the "Lyrical Ballads"* (Berkeley: University of California Press, 1976).

3   I discuss Romantic defamiliarizing at length in *British Romantic Art* (Berkeley: University of California Press, 1986).

4   These characteristics Todorov refers to in comments on transience and hesitation in the fantastic, although, as I have noted, his remarks tend to obscure the fact that the uncertainty provoked by fantasy is irresolvable.

5   *Specimens of Table Talk of the Late Samuel Taylor Coleridge*, ed. H. N. Coleridge, 2 vols. (London: John Murray, 1835), 2:155–56. Edward W. Lane, in the standard translation of *The Thousand and One Nights* (London: Chatto and Windus, 1912), 3 vols., 1:53, notes that dates have no shells, and that the merchant is culpable for not have exclaimed "Destoor!" when throwing aside the date stone, which, in fact, killed (rather than blinded) the Djinn's son.

6   There is a substantial body of commentary on the poem and its origin, much of the most pertinent cited by Utley and McGann in the essays mentioned in note 9 below. The journal letter to George and Georgiana Keats appears in *The Letters of John Keats*, ed. Hyder E. Rollins, 2 vols. 2:58–109 (Cambridge, Mass.: Harvard University Press, 1958), (quotations from this work are cited in my text as Rollins with page number, with volume number given only for volume one). The textual history of the poem is given by Jack Stillinger, *The Texts of Keats's Poems* (Cambridge, Mass.: Harvard University Press, 1974), 232–34, and Stillinger in his superb edition of the *Poems* (Cambridge, Mass.: Harvard University Press, 1978), 357–59, prints the so-called Brown version, and is the source for my

text printed in note 10 of this chapter. In the "Editorial Commentary" of *Essays in Criticism* 4, 4 (1954): 432–40, Kenneth Muir and F. W. Bateson, through a discussion of Robert Gittings' then recent book, *John Keats: The Living Year*, raise several significant issues involved in the speculations as to the inspiration of "La Belle Dame," including the possible relation of Keats's ballad to Wordsworth's work. J. M. Sinclair, "When is a Poem Like a Sunset" in *Ballad Studies*, ed. E. B. Lyle (Cambridge: P. S. Breur, 1976) reports an interesting experiment on changes made in the poem by students who some time after memorizing the ballad wrote it down. The pattern of errors resulting illuminate the intricacy of Keats's simple-seeming art.

7   Rosemary Jackson, *Fantasy: The Literature of Subversion* (London: Methuen, 1981), 26. Congruent with Jackson's approach is that of Fredric Jameson, *The Political Unconscious: Narrative as Socially Symbolic Act* (Ithaca: Cornell University Press, 1981). Jameson sees magical narratives in modern capitalistic cultures as providing "freedom from that reality principle to which a now oppressive realistic representation is the hostage" (104). Other commentators on fantasy led by their analyses to descriptions paralleling Keats's definition of negative capability include Brooke-Rose, Swinfer, and Manlove, whose works are cited in notes to chapter 1. Kathyrn Hume in *Fantasy and Mimesis* (New York: Methuen, 1984), a work synthesizing the ideas of her predecessors, argues that a survey of the major studies proves that appreciation of the fantastic in literature is enhanced when one approaches the subject through broad, inclusive definitions rather than exclusive, narrowly limiting ones (20–22). Tobin Siebers, who perceives the fantastic as a major vehicle in the Romantic aesthetic's rejection of Enlightenment principles, cites a wide range of European Romantic writers who shared Keats's preference for "poetic pluralism in the face of what they believed to be a singleminded and restrictive mentality" (*The Romantic Fantastic*, 26). See also note 7, chapter 6 below. Intriguing also, though beyond the scope of this work, are possible connections between negative capability and Heidegger's term *Gelassenheit* (which is derived from Meister Eckhart), usually translated as "releasement," a kind of unwilled thinking, which Heidegger links to *Edelmut*, nobleness of mind, mind capable of openness to mystery. See Martin Heidegger, *Discourse on Thinking: A Translation of Gelassenheit*, trans. John M. Anderson and E. Hans Freund (New York: Harper, Torchbook, 1966), especially p. 64.

8 Charles Lamb, "Imperfect Sympathies," *The Works of Charles and Mary Lamb*, ed. E. V. Lucas, 10 vols. (London: Methuen, 1903), 2:60.

9 Francis Lee Utley, "The Infernos of Lucretius and of Keats's "La Belle Dame Sans Merci," *ELH* 25 (1958): 105–21; Jerome J. McGann, "Keats and the Historical Method in Literary Criticism," *Modern Language Notes* 94 (1979), 988–1032. It is a pity McGann apparently was unaware of Utley's essay, for the earlier work might have enabled him to define more sharply the critical issues he wishes to raise. Another analysis unfortunately slighted by McGann is that of Charles I. Patterson, Jr., in his *The Daemonic in the Poetry of John Keats* (Urbana: University of Illinois Press, 1970), 125–50, especially good on the lady as "neutral to good and evil" because "outside the human pale" (138), and on such details as the problem of the antecedent for "this" in stanza 12.

10 Earl Wasserman, *The Finer Tone: Keats's Major Poems* (Baltimore: Johns Hopkins University Press, 1952), 63–83. Wasserman's careful analysis is interesting in several respects, not least for arguing that the ballad is a preparation for the great odes written in the next month, especially the "Ode on a Grecian Urn," a possibility to which I refer in chapter 6. But for me the ballad, like the "Ode to Psyche," is significant for its indeterminacies, its negative capability, whereas Wasserman praises Keats, as Warren praises Coleridge in "The Ancient Mariner," for conceiving of a poem as "a perfectly ordered cosmos, an experience not only completed but also self-centered by reason of . . . perfect circularity." (82)

The Brown and *Indicator* texts follow.

The Brown transcript of *La Belle Dame sans Merci:*

A Ballad

1

O what can ail thee, knight at arms,
    Alone and palely loitering?
The sedge has wither'd from the lake,
    And no birds sing.

2

O what can ail thee, knight at arms,
    So haggard and so woe-begone?
The squirrel's granary is full,
    And the harvest's done.

3

I see a lily on thy brow
    With anguish moist and fever dew,
And on thy cheeks a fading rose
    Fast withereth too.

4

I met a lady in the meads,
    Full beautiful, a fairy's child;
Her hair was long, her foot was light,
    And her eyes were wild.

5

I made a garland for her head,
    And bracelets too, and fragrant zone;
She look'd at me as she did love,
    And made sweet moan.

6

I set her on my pacing steed,
    And nothing else saw all day long,
For sidelong would she bend, and sing
    A fairy's song.

7

She found me roots of relish sweet,
    And honey wild, and manna dew,
And sure in language strange she said—
    I love thee true.

8

She took me to her elfin grot,
    And there she wept, and sigh'd full sore,
And there I shut her wild wild eyes
    With kisses four.

9

And there she lulled me asleep,
    And there I dream'd—Ah! woe betide!
The latest dream I ever dream'd
    On the cold hill's side.

10

I saw pale kings, and princes too,
    Pale warriors, death pale were they all;
They cried—"La belle dame sans merci
    Hath thee in thrall!"

11

I saw their starv'd lips in the gloam,
    With horrid warning gaped wide,
And I awoke and found me here
    On the cold hill's side.

12

And this is why I sojurn here,
    Alone and palely loitering,
Though the sedge is wither'd from the lake,
    And no birds sing.

The Poems of John Keats, ed. Jack Stillinger
[Cambridge, Mass.: Harvard University Press, 1978], 357–59.

The Indicator version of *"La Belle Dame sans Merci"*

Ah, what can ail thee, wretched wight,
    Alone and palely loitering;
The sedge is withered from the lake,
    And no birds sing.

Ah, what can ail thee, wretched wight,
    So haggard and so woe-begone?
The squirrel's granary is full,
    And the harvest's done.

I see a lily on thy brow.
    With anguish moist and fever dew;
And on they cheek a fading rose
    Fast withereth too.

I met a Lady in the meads
    Full beautiful, a fairy's child;
Her hair was long, her foot was light,
    And her eyes were wild.

I set her on my pacing steed,
    And nothing else saw all day long;
For sideways would she lean, and sing
    A fairy's song.

I made a garland for her head,
    And bracelets too, and fragrant zone;
She looked at me as she did love,
    And made sweet moan.

She found me roots of relish sweet,
    And honey wild, and manna dew;
And sure in language strange she said,
    I love thee true.

She took me to her elfin grot,
    And there she gazed and sighed deep,
And there I shut her wild sad eyes—
    So kissed to sleep.

And there we slumbered on the moss,
    And there I dreamed—ah, woe betide—
The latest dream I ever dreamed
    On the cold hill side.

I saw pale kings, and princes too,
    Pale warriors, death-pale were they all;
Who cried—"La belle Dame sans mercy
    Hath thee in thrall!"

I saw their starved lips in the gloom
    With horrid warning gapèd wide,
And I awoke and found me here
    On the cold hill side.

And this is why I sojurn here
    Alone and palely loitering
Though the sedge is withered from the lake,
    And no birds sing.

                              The Poems of John Keats, ed. Miriam Allott.
                              [London: Longman, 1970], 757–58.

11 Anonymous critic of 1849 cited in G. M. Matthews, *Keats: The
    Critical Heritage* (New York: Barnes & Noble, 1971), 345.

CHAPTER 4

1   Albert B. Friedman, *The Ballad Revival: Studies in the Influence of Popular on Sophisticated Poetry* (Princeton: Princeton University Press, 1961), stresses this point, citing "The Ancient Mariner" to exemplify "how unlike the ballads in radical respects a ballad can be and yet rightly convince us that without the ballads it could not have been conceived" (277–78).

2   I, to the contrary, find the most interesting "late" balladeer to be Swinburne, who was profoundly attracted to the form and whose ear for traditional nuances of diction and rhythm was acute— trained perhaps by his having heard ballads recited in his youth. The faults in his ballads arise from a too faithful imitating of authentic conventions. One of his finest ballads, "Duriesdyke," written in 1859, only became generally available twenty years ago through the editorial efforts of Anne Henry Ehrenpreis, *The Literary Ballad* (London: Edward Arnold, 1966), 166–70.

3   William Wordsworth, *The Poetical Works*, 2d ed., ed. Ernest de Selincourt and Helen Darbishire, 5 vols. (Oxford: Clarendon Press, 1952–59) 2:331. In the Advertisement to the *Lyrical Ballads* of 1798 the ballad was specifically singled out as "founded on well authenticated fact."

4   *The Poetical Works*, 4:439–40. For Darwin's influence, see James H. Averill, "Wordsworth and Modern Science: The Poetry of 1798," *Journal of English and Germanic Philology* 77 (1978), 232–46. John K. Primeau, "The Influence of G. D. Burger on the 'Lyrical Ballads' of William Wordsworth: The Supernatural vs. the Natural," *Germanic Review* 58, 3 (1983): 89–96, emphasizes in particular "The Idiot Boy" as a deliberate burlesque of the supernaturalism in "Lenore" and "Der Wilde Jager."

5   William Southey, *Critical Review*, 2d series, 24 (October 1798): 197–04, cited from *The Romantics Reviewed*, ed. Donald H. Reiman (New York: Garland, 1972), part A, 1:305.

6   Reverend Burney, *The Monthly Review*, 2d series, 29 (June 1799): 206–07, cited from *The Romantics Reviewed*, part A, 1:715.

7   *Poetical Works*, 2:401.

8   *The Complete Poetry and Prose of William Blake*, rev. ed., ed. David V. Erdman (Berkeley: University of California Press, 1982), 488–89

9   Tobin Siebers, *The Romantic Fantastic*, (Ithaca: Cornell University Press, 1984), 29. Blake and Wordsworth in different ways represent suffering caused by progress, whereas Coleridge and Keats return

the reader to a superstitiousness scorned by progressive minds, but all these Romantic poets sympathetically adopt the viewpoint of the victims, rather than of the victors, of enlightened social and intellectual advances. Hugh Honour, *Romanticism* (New York: Harper, 1979), 34–35, describes cogently this phenomenon of depiction from the victim's position in the paintings of Antoine-Jean Gros, Turner, and Goya.

10   Shakespeare's exploitation of fantastic elements is not, of course, confined to the few plays I have mentioned; see the excellent essay by Peter Malekin, "Shakespeare, Freedom, and the Fantastic," in *Forms of the Fantastic*, ed. Jan Hokenson and Howard Pearce (New York: Greenwood Press, 1986), 129–42, particularly good on fantastic elements in *Hamlet* and *Lear*. I also move briskly past a host of complexities concerning the Romantic poets' relations to popular beliefs and popular forms, perhaps the most significant of which are connected with the drama. I am inclined to believe that some part of the Romantics' admiration for Shakespeare's fantasy derives from their difficulties with his more realistic comedy. An important essay on dramatic comedy in the romantic era is that of Michael Hays, "Comedy as Being/Comedy as Idea," *Studies in Romanticism* 26 (Summer 1987): 211–30.

11   I cite Walter Scott's version in *The Minstrelsy of the Scottish Border*, rev. and ed. by T. F. Henderson, 4 vols. (Edinburgh: Oliver and Boyd, 1932), 3:246–52.

12   Again I cite from Henderson's edition of Scott's *Minstrelsy*, 4:86–90. Earl Wasserman's remark in *The Finer Tone*, p. 68, that this version "differs in a few important details" from that available to Keats in Robert Jamieson's *Popular Ballads* of 1806, is a staggering understatement. We know Keats knew Scott's work, and it seems certain that his version was at the least one of the sources of Keats's acquaintance with True Thomas.

13   J. R. R. Tolkien, "On Fairy Stories," *The Tolkien Reader* (New York: Ballantine, 1966), 5.

CHAPTER 5

1   "The Rime of the Ancient Mariner," lines 190–194, *The Poems of Samuel Taylor Coleridge*, ed. E. H. Coleridge (London: Oxford University Press, 1960), 194. All references to the poem hereafter are cited in the text by line number in this edition, which contains full apparatus on changes in the text of the poem, including modifications such as that of line 194 to the catachretic "And she was far liker Death than he," that I use as an epigraph to chapter 7. I

touch but lightly in my discussion on such changes without doing justice to their significance,which deserves more attention than they have yet received, though see note 6 below. My citations from "Childe Roland to the Dark Tower Came," are from *Poems of Robert Browning*, ed. Donald Smalley (Boston: Houghton-Mifflin, 1956), 162–68.

2   John Livingston Lowes, *The Road to Xanadu: A Study in the Ways of the Imagination*, 2d ed. (New York: Knopf, 1930).

3   Arnold E. Davidson, "The Concluding Moral in Coleridge's *The Rime of the Ancient Mariner*," *Philological Quarterly* 60, 1 (1981): 87–93, is one of the later analyses of the moral's inadequacies, which were earlier discussed by Gayle S. Smith in "A Reappraisal of the Moral Stanzas in 'The Rime of the Ancient Mariner,'" *Studies in Romanticism* 3, 1 (1963), while even before Warren, wrote, Newton P. Stallknecht concentrated his interpretation on this issue in "The Moral of 'The Ancient Mariner,'" *PMLA* 47 (1932): 560–69.

4   Robert Penn Warren, "A Poem of Pure Imagination," *Selected Essays* (New York: Knopf, Vintage, 1966), 198–305; further citations in my text refer to this edition as SE with page number. In its original and shorter form Warren's essay first appeared in *The Kenyon Review* 8, 3 (1946): 391–427, with illustrations manifesting admirably the modern concept of primitivism which has contaminated twentieth-century appreciation of fantasy.

5   For example. Homer Obed Brown, "The Art of Theology and the Theology of Art: R. P. Warren's Reading of Coleridge's *The Rime of the Ancient Mariner*," *Boundary* 2 8, 1 (Fall 1979): 237–60, and the following essay in this issue by Jonathan Arac, "Repetition and Exclusion: Coleridge and the New Criticism Reconsidered," 261–73, which uses Brown's study to plot admirably the history of *Mariner* criticism.

6   E. E. Bostetter, *The Romantic Ventriloquists* (Seattle: University of Washington Press, 1963), 114, 115, 118. Raimonda Modiano develops the same kind of skeptical approach in "Words and 'Languageless' Meanings: Limits of Expression in *The Rime of the Ancient Mariner*," *Modern Language Quarterly* 38 (1977).

7   Among those who have studied the gloss with attention to its functions are Huntington Brown, "The Gloss to *The Rime of the Ancient Mariner*," *Modern Language Quarterly* 6 (1945): 319–24, L. M. Grow, "The Search for Truth: Book Learning Versus Personal Experience in 'The Rime of the Ancient Mariner,'" *Coranto* 10, 2 (1977): 3–10, and more recently K. M. Wheeler, *The Creative Mind in Coleridge's Poetry* (London: Heinemann, 1981), 51–64, which includes full references to other earlier studies,

including an important essay by Lawrence Lipking, "The Marginal Gloss," *Critical Inquiry* 3 (1977): 609–55, that considers "glossing" in a wide context. Another late addition is the epigraph from Thomas Burnet, which was published only in 1817. The importance of the changes in title, epigraph, and text of the ballad have only recently begun to attract the critical attention they deserve—for example what *gloss* meant to Coleridge: see Wheeler above, as well as the earlier articles by Irene H. Chayes, "A Coleridgean Reading of 'The Ancient Mariner,'" *Studies in Romanticism* 4 (1965): 81–103, and J. Robert Barth, *The Symbolic Imagination: Coleridge and the Romantic Tradition* (Princeton; Princeton University Press, 1977), 97–104.

8   Irving Babbitt, "The Problem of the Imagination: Coleridge," *On Being Creative and Other Essays* (Boston: Houghton Mifflin, 1932), 97–133, 120.

9   Jonathan Culler, "Literary Fantasy," *The Cambridge Review* 95 (1973): 30–33, 33.

10 *Specimens of Table Talk of the Late Samuel Taylor Coleridge*, ed. H. N. Coleridge, 2 vols. (London: John Murray, 1835), 2:155–56. Warren begins his essay with a discussion of this celebrated passage, but Arac is the first commentator I know to observe that the story to which Coleridge refers is at the beginning of *The Arabian Nights*, and that in it the merchant is finally saved by the telling of marvelous stories. "Narrative meaning," not "meaninglessness," that is to say, meaning articulable only through narrative telling, is that to which Coleridge's parable points. See note 13 below for Tobin Siebers' recent essay on "storytelling" as a crux of Hoffmann's "The Sandman," a crux ignored by Freud and critics of "The Uncanny" alike.

11 Louis Vax, *Le Séduction de l'étrange* (Paris: Presses Universitaire, 1965), ascribes to this shifting between "le profond et le superficiel" the fact that "la metaphysique du fantastique torne si aisément à la métaphysique fantastique!" (246).

12 Arden Reed, *Romantic Weather* (Hanover: University Press of New England, 1983), 147–81, see esp. 172–73.

13 Sigmund Freud, *Studies in Parapsychology* (New York: Collier, 1963), 37. Throughout my quotations are from this easily available edition, identified by F with page number; the essay, which first appeared in 1919, may be found in volume 17 of the *The Standard Edition* (London: Hogarth, 1953–62). Among the most useful studies of "The Uncanny" are one forthcoming by Tobin Siebers, "'Those Hideous Voice is This?' The Romantic Fantastic in Freud

and Hoffman," *New Orleans Review* 15, (1988), and earlier in chapter 5 of *The Mirror of Medusa* (Berkeley: University of California Press, 1983) as well as in chapter 1 of *The Romantic Fantastic* (Ithaca: Cornell University Press, 1985). Hélène Cixous, "Fiction and its Phantoms: A Reading of Freud's *Das Unheimliche* (The 'Uncanny')," *New Literary History* 7 (1976) 525–48, and Neil Hertz, "Freud and the 'Sandman,'" in *Textual Strategies*, ed. Josue Harrari (Ithaca: Cornell University Press, 1979), 296–321. Hertz is especially to be recommended for his comments on the place of the essay in Freud's career. Both Hertz and Cixous comment cogently on Freud's drastic deformations of Hoffmann's story in both his retellings of it, the second in a long footnote, which, as Hertz observes, though it concludes with a glancing remark on Hoffman's biography, is primarily directed at insisting on the universality of the castration-complex. Siebers' most recent essay is the first to call attention to Freud's ignoring (an oversight continued by commentators on his work) that Nathanael, the protagonist of Hoffmann's story, is a would-be writer of Romantic tales, that, indeed, his "masterpiece" is in essence the plot of "The Sandman."

The intricacies of Freud's various works that touch on my topic that I cannot take space here to discuss adequately may be suggested by his essay "Dreams and Occultism" (appearing in *Studies in Parapsychology*), which details his conviction of the reality of mental telepathy. From the perspective of anyone interested in the fate of fantasy in our century, Freud's most significant contribution was probably his defining of the unconscious as the repository of otherness, thus adroitly absorbing into the human psyche many forces that previously had been regarded as external to humankind. The significance of this move is dramatized by Lacan's logical development of it in associating the unconscious with language, the distinctively human capability.

14 Hal Foster, "The 'Primitive' Unconscious of Modern Art," *October* 34 (Fall 1985): 45–70, 60. Foster's essay is one of several recent explorations into the centrality of the concept of primitivism in modern Western culture and art, many triggered by the exhibition and accompanying two-volume study mounted by the Museum of Modern Art in 1984. A penetrating analysis of this exhibition (and associated events) is provided by James Clifford, "Histories of the Tribal and the Modern," *Modern America* 73 (April 1985): 164–215. Clifford observes how impressively the displays at the Museum of Modern Art and the accompanying catalogue represents Modernism as a discovery of universal ahistorical principles transcending

cultural differences (166), thereby effectively diminishing the ectypal historicity of the tribal artifacts that were supposedly being
celebrated.

CHAPTER 6

1   Journal-letter of February 14–May 3, 1819, to George and Geor-
    giana Keats, April 30, *The Letters of John Keats*, ed. Hyder E.
    Rollins, 2 vols. (Cambridge, Mass.: Harvard University Press, 1958),
    2: 105.
2   Keats knew *The Golden Ass* through William Adlington's translation
    of 1566—the lines in the ode describing Psyche couched in flowers
    and bedded grass seems derived from Adlington's description of her
    "couched among the soft and tender hearbs [*sic*], as in a bed of
    sweet and fragrant flowers." My citations, however, are from the
    translation of *The Golden Ass* by Jack Lindsay (Bloomington:
    Indiana University Press, 1960), because this is the only English
    version I have found that does any justice to the ornateness of
    Apuleius' style. Citations in my text from this edition are identified
    by A and page number.
3   Lines 141–50, *The Poems of John Keats*, ed. Jack Stillinger (Cam-
    bridge, Mass.: Harvard University Press, 1978), 84. All my quota-
    tions from "The Ode to Psyche" and "The Fall of Hyperion" are
    from this edition, the poems appearing, respectively, on 364–67 and
    478–91.
4   Fred Licht, *Canova* (New York: Abbeville Publishers, 1984), 164.
5   Ian Jack in *Keats and the Mirror of Art* (Oxford: Clarendon, 1967)
    describes in detail the relation of Keats's ode to possible sources
    both in literature and the fine arts, finding the poem to be
    "essentially a pagan act of worship" (204). An excellent analysis of
    the ode appears in Stuart Sperry's *Keats the Poet* (Princeton:
    Princeton University Press, 1973), 249–61, especially valuable for
    connecting "shadowy thought" with negative capability and
    suggesting ways in which this "early" ode points to the deeper
    complexities of "Lamia." I might here note that some problems of
    reading Keats's odes as forming a definite progression are effectively
    highlighted by Robert Gleckner, "Keats's Odes: The Problems of the
    Limited Canon," *Studies in English Literature* 5, 4 (1965): 577–85.
    Helen Vendler's discussion of "The Ode to Psyche" in her recent
    The Odes of John Keats (Cambridge, Mass.: Harvard University
    Press, 1983), 47–70, calls Keats's art in this ode "the insubstantial
    one of Fancy, the inner activity of the working brain, not even, as

yet, the art of poetry embodied in words" (48), though she credits Keats in this poem with resisting even more debilitating tendencies toward "emblematic allegory."

6 C. W. Hagelman, Jr., "Keats's Medical Training and the Last Stanza of the 'Ode to Psyche,' " *Keats-Shelley Journal* 11 (1962): 73–82.

7 It seems to me significant that several recent feminist critics have celebrated Keats's "feminine qualities," which they associate with negative capability, for example, Erica Jong, "Visionary Anger," *Ms* 11 (July 1973), Margaret Homans, *Women Writers and Poetic Identity* (Princeton: Princeton University Press, 1980), esp. 240n25, and Adrienne Rich, "Three Conversations," in *Adrienne Rich's Poetry: Texts of the Poems, the Poet on Her Work, Reviews, and Criticism*, ed. Barbara Charlesworth Gelpi and Albert Gelpi (New York: Norton, 1975).

8 I have treated this topic extensively in *British Romantic Art* (Berkeley: University of California Press, 1986), chapter 4.

9 *The Notebooks of Samuel Taylor Coleridge*, ed. Kathleen Coburn (Princeton: Princeton University Press, 1973), vol. 3, part 1, note 3268.

10 C. N. Manlove, *Modern Fantasy: Five Studies* (Cambridge: Cambridge University Press, 1975), 5.

11 T. E. Apter, *Fantasy Literature* (Bloomington: Indiana University Press, 1982), 3.

12 In my simplified contrast between Romantic imaginative psychology and Modern scientific psychology are implicated a vast complex of ideas, especially those of play, eroticism, and pleasure, as is sensitively demonstrated by Michael G. Cooke in "Romanticism: Pleasure and Play," *The Age of William Wordsworth*, eds. Kenneth R. Johnston and Gene W. Ruoff (New Brunswick: Rutgers University Press, 1987), 62–83. Cooke observes, for example, that Romantic psychology allowed for "enobled" concepts of play and pleasure, whereas, "if we then consider the interpretation of art in the psychoanalytic tradition the opposition comes out graphically"—as is illustrated by a contemporary psychologist who sees play beginning "only when the child realizes the difference between killing a father doll and killing a father" (77–78).

13 Lord Dunsany, *Gods, Men and Ghosts*, ed. E. F. Bleiler (New York: Dover, 1972), "The Sword of Welleran," 102–115, 103; subsequent quotations are identified by page number in my text. I feel some discomfort in speaking slightingly of Dunsany's writing, which has given me much pleasure, and the range of whose virtues is currently

little appreciated. Several of his plays are dramatically effective, his fictional representation of the disasterous effects of religious conflict in modern-day Ireland is agonizingly acute, and his descriptions of hunting in Africa are to my mind superior to Hemingway's.

CHAPTER 7

1   All my citations from Kleist's fiction (indicated in the text by MK and page number) are from *The Marquise of O and Other Stories,* trans. David Luke and Nigel Reeves (Harmondsworth: Penguin, 1978); their comments on *Kohlhaas* which I have quoted appear on pages 27 and 28. Kleist's use of history for "fantastic" purposes is, in fact, paralleled by Sir Walter Scott, most impressively in two short stories, "The Highland Widow" and "The Two Drovers." Throughout his novels Scott presents antiquated superstitions in a fashion subversive of conventional, enlightened skepticism. A discussion of this feature of Scott's art with references to others who have examined it appears in my *British Romantic Art* (Berkeley: University of California Press, 1985), 115–16.

Readers without German may consult a recent essay treating *Kohlhaas* as "a truly philosophical narrative" by Richard Kuhns, "The Strangeness of Justice: Reading *Michael Kohlhass,*" *New Literary History* 15 (1983): 73–91. Ilse Graham's *Heinrich von Kleist: Word Into Flesh. A Poet's Quest for the Symbol* (Berlin: Walter de Gruyter, 1977) is a valuable study based on careful analyses of the texts, cited in both the original and translation, with chapter 12 devoted to *Kohlhaas.* Walter Silz, *Heinrich von Kleist: Studies in His Works and Literary Character* (Philadelphia: University of Pennsylvania Press, 1961), chapter 6, provides a fine reading of *Kohlhaas* based on a detailed description of the novella's second paragraph, beginning,

> with its slightly over four octavo pages, as printed in the standard edition, it is not much above the average length for a paragraph in *Kohlhaas.* Its very first lines are a good example of the Kleistian sentence, with a strong main stem to which additional modifying elements are attached, as it were, by pegs of commas, and with its central colon marking the turning point.(173).

Were I to provide a thorough analysis of the novella I should have to take into account the density of such stylistic minutiae, but that would require discussion of the original text, not a translation. Also worth attention is John Ellis, *Heinrich von Kleist: Studies in the Character and Meaning of his Writing* (Chapel Hill: University of North Carolina Press, 1970) and his subsequent *Narration in the German Novelle* (Cambridge: Cambridge University Press, 1974).

2 Gabriel García Márquez, "Latin America's Impossible Reality," trans. Elena Brunet, *Harpers Magazine* (January 1985): 13–16, 13. The essay previously appeared in *Sabádo*, the weekend supplement to the Mexican newspaper *Unomásuno*, August 4, 1984. The second quotation is from 15.

3 Gabriel García Márquez, *Leaf Storm and Other Stories*, trans. Gregory Rabassa (New York: Avon, 1973), 187–96, 190, all subsequent quotations are from this text. Anyone who compares the original, available as "El Último Viaje del Buque Fantasmo" in *Siete Cuentos* (Buenos Aires: Editorial Sudamerica, 1972) will I'm sure be dazzled by the accuracy and fluency of Rabassa's translation.

There is now a vast body of commentary of García Márquez' writing and on "magic realism," a term invented by the German art critic Franz Roh in 1924. An amplified version of Roh's work in the Spanish translation of 1927 is now available in English, *German Art in the Twentieth Century* (Greenwich, Conn.: New York Graphic Society, 1968). Worth consulting are Luis Leal, "El realismo mágico en las literature hispanoamericana," *Cuadernos Americanos* 153, 4 (July–August, 1967): 230–35, and Lorraine Elena Ben-Ur, "El Realismo mágico en la critica hispanoamerica," *Journal of Spanish Studies* 4, 3 (Winter 1976): 149–63, and the minor but often cited essay of Angel Flores, "Magical Realism in Spanish American Fiction," *Hispanica* 38, 2 (1955): 187–92). But all these should be considered in the light of the sardonic analysis of Emir Rodriquez Monegal, "Realismo mágico versus literatura fantástica: un diálogo de sordos," in *Otros Mundos: Otros Fuegos: fantasia y realism mágico in Iberoameárica*, Memoria del 16 Congreso Internacional de Literatura Iberoamericana, ed. Donald A. Yates (East Lansing: Michigan State University Latin American Studies Center, 1975), 25–37, a volume including several other essays relevant to the topic.

Rodriguez Monegal, besides demonstrating the shortcomings of some of the critical scholarship of others who have studied the relation of magical realism and fantasy, articulates with lucidity the differences between diverse practitioners of the former which would have to be taken into account were one satisfactorily to describe the relation of one phenomenon to the other. He shows how Roh's original definition was formulated to describe an aesthetic movement reacting against Expressionism, and makes the interesting suggestion that Carpentier's "concepcion de 'lo real marvilloso' constituye tambien una *reaccion*, contra lo maravilloso surrealista" (31). On the latter, one may consult the chapter entitled "The Enchanters' Domain" in J. H. Matthews, *An Introduction to Surrealism* (University Park: Pennsylvania State University Press, 1965). More recently Amaryll Beatrice Chanady, *Magical Realism and the Fantastic: Resolved Versus Unresolved Antinomy* (New York: Garland, 1985), has touched on these topics, but without effectively deepening our insight. There seems to be no really satisfactory study of the relation or non-relation of "magical realism" to surrealism. I was disappointed, for example, to find Anna Balakian in her most recent edition (the 3d) of *Surrealism: The Road to the Absolute* (Chicago: University of Chicago Press, 1986) continuing to ignore Latin America and pointing to only relatively minor effects of the surrealist movement in North America. Until we fully understand how surrealism contributed, both positively and negatively, to later literary developments outside of France and among nonmainstream writers, Baraka, for example, it is virtually impossible satisfactorily to account for connections to and differences from recent literary fantasy and earlier art in this mode. Perhaps the solution of Jaime Alazraki to denominate recent works as "neofantastic" to suggest both their relation to and distance from their nineteenth-century predecessors is for now the best available: see his "The Fantastic as Surrealist Metaphors in Cortazar's Short Fiction," *Dada/Surrealism* 5 (1975): 28–33, and his "Introduction: Toward the Last Square of the Hopscotch," *The Final Island: The Fiction of Julio Cortazar*, eds. Jaime Alazraki and Ivar Ivask (Norman: University of Oklahoma Press, 1976), 3–18.

4 Kleist's stylistic complexity is difficult to render in translation, particularly the fashion in which he makes syntax constitute plot. Ilse Graham (219) cites an example which, because most of the sentence consists in titles and proper names, may be comprehensible to an English reader. Luther's letter to the Saxon Elector is received in the fashion described by the following sentence:

> Der Kurfurst erhielt diesen Brief *eben* [The Elector received this letter *at the moment that*] als der Prinz Christiern von Meissen, Generalissimus des Reichs, Oheim des bei Mulheim geschlageneen und an seinen Wunden noch daniederliegenden Prinzen Friedrich von Meissen; [when Prince Christiern of Meissen, Commander in Chief of the realm, uncle of Prince Friedrich of Meissen who had been

routed at Mulheim and was still bedridden with his wounds] der Grosskanzler des Tribunals, Graf Wrede; Graf Kallheim, Prasident der Staatskanzlei; und die beiden Herren Hinz und Kunz von Tronka, dieser Kammerer, jenr Mundschenck, die Jugendfreunde und Vertrauten des Herrn, in dem Schlosse *gegenwartig waren.* [the Grand Chancellor of the Courts of State, Count Wrede; Count Kallheim, President of the Chancery of State; and the two lords Hinz and Kunz of Tronka, the latter chamberlain, the former cupbearer, both his highness' boyhood friends and confidants, at the castle *were present.*]

The bureaucracy, most of it ill disposed because related or politically connected to the Junker von Tronka who is Kohlhaas' enemy, that encircles the Elector and assures that the effect of Luther's missive will be diffused if not warped, is dramatically represented by their titles syntactically crowding in between the moment of reception of the letter and the completion of the sentence with its suspended verb, a completion that is almost redundant, since it affirms verbally what we have already *felt* through the listing of names, positions, and titles that form the encircling presence.

5 Clifford Geertz, *Negara* (Princeton: Princeton University Press, 1980), 122, 123.

Index